FOR ORGANS, PIANOS & ELECTRONIC KEYBOARDS

E-Z PLAY TODAY

66

LA LA LAND

MUSIC FROM MOTION PICTURE

ISBN 978-1-4950-9275-6

HAL•LEONARD®
7777 W. BLUEMOUND RD. P.O. BOX 13819 MILWAUKEE, WI 53213

In Australia Contact:
Hal Leonard Australia Pty. Ltd.
4 Lentara Court
Cheltenham, Victoria, 3192 Australia
Email: ausadmin@halleonard.com.au

Another Day of Sun

Registration 2
Rhythm: Swing

Music by Justin Hurwitz
Lyrics by Benj Pasek & Justin Paul

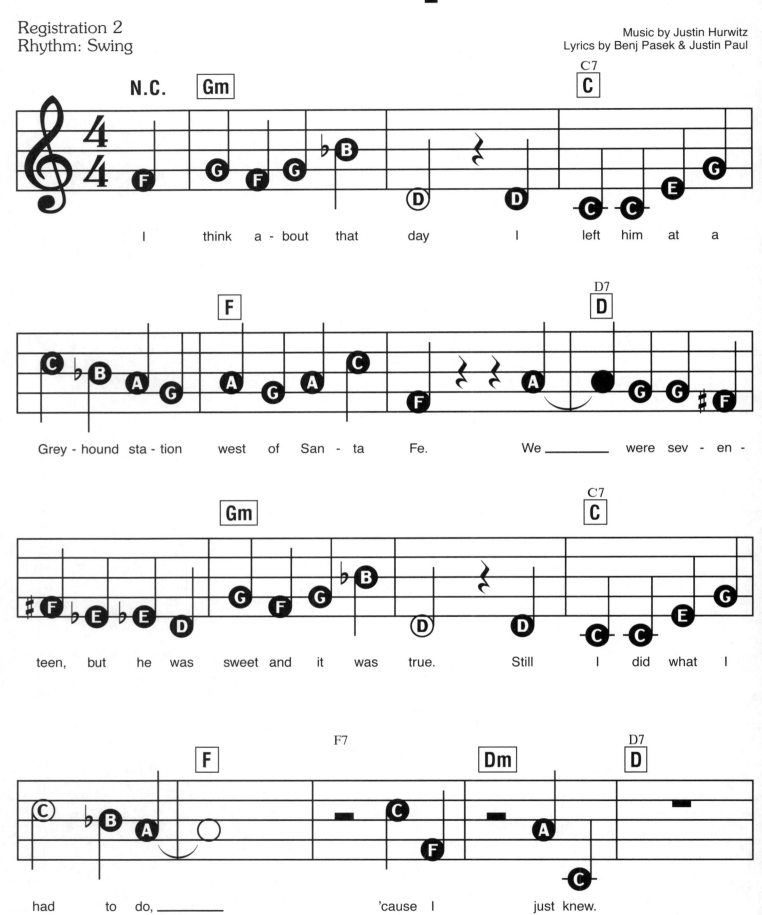

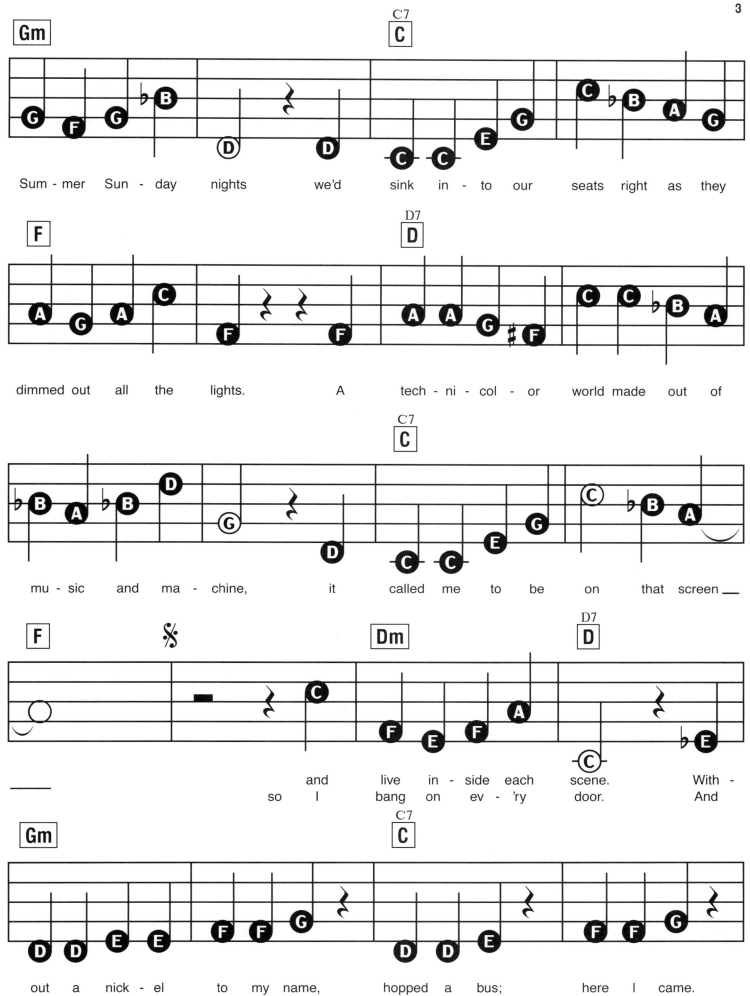

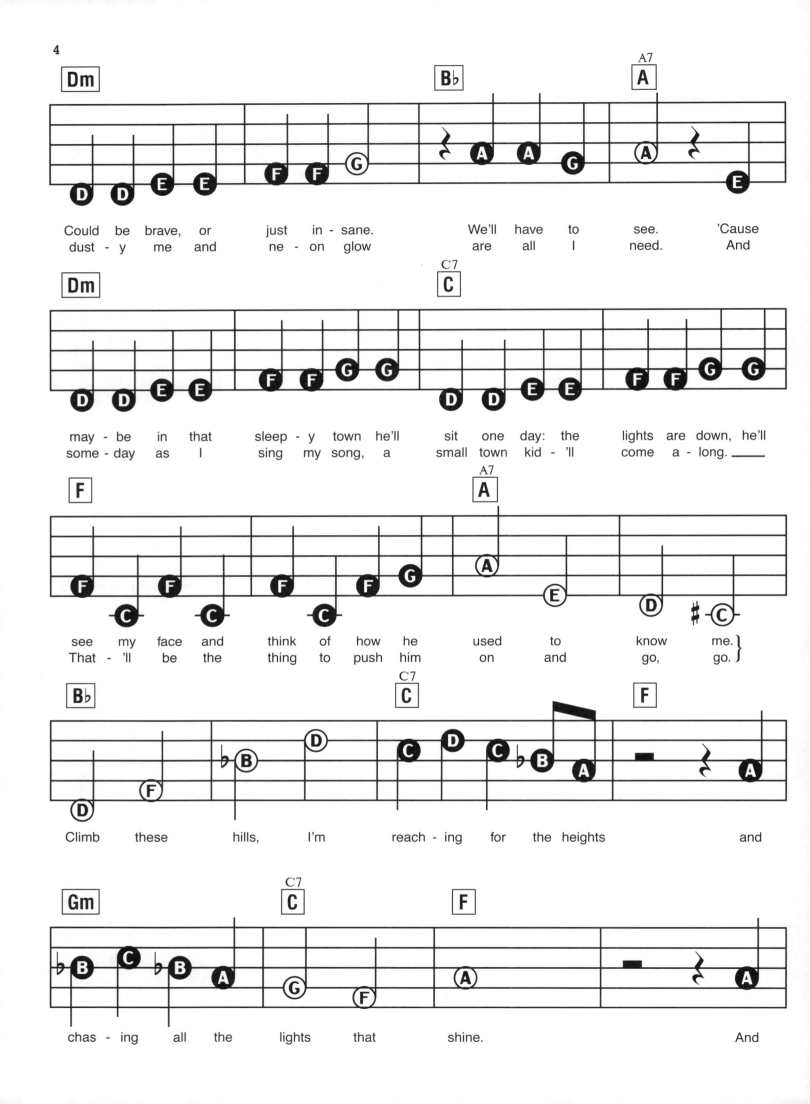

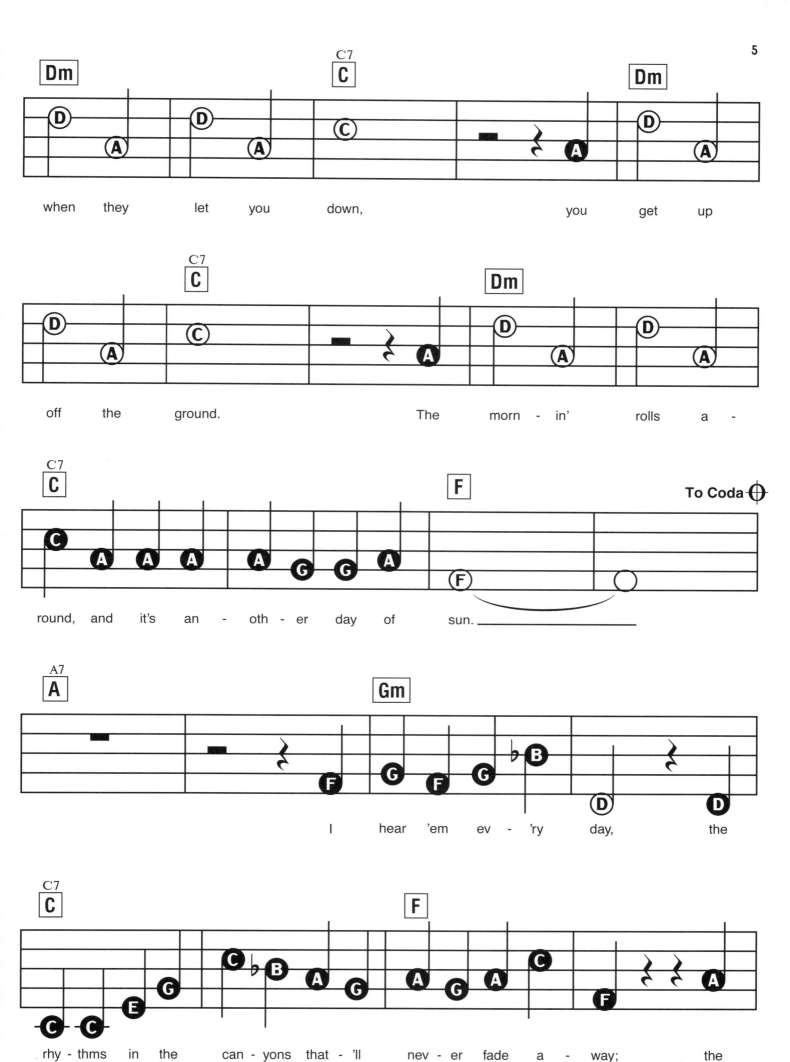

6

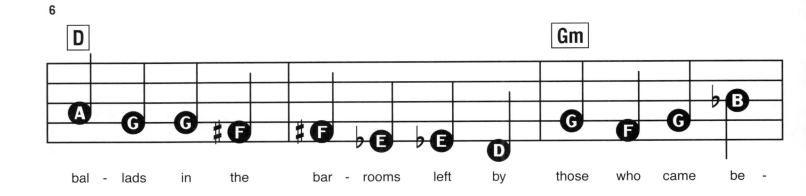

bal - lads in the bar - rooms left by those who came be -

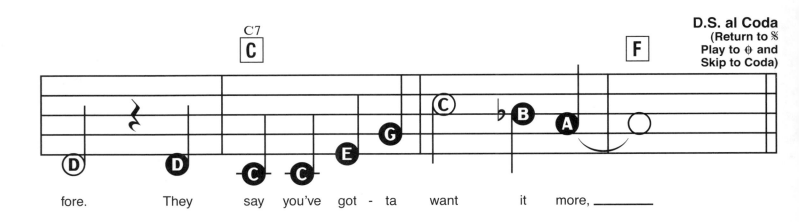

D.S. al Coda
(Return to 𝄋
Play to ⊕ and
Skip to Coda)

fore. They say you've got - ta want it more, _____

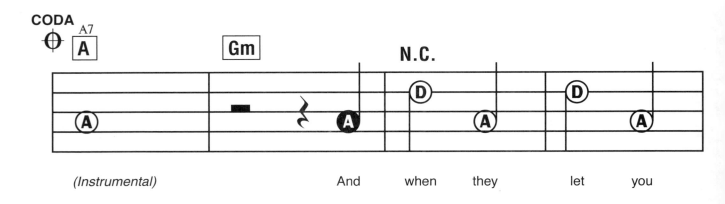

CODA

(Instrumental)   And when they let you

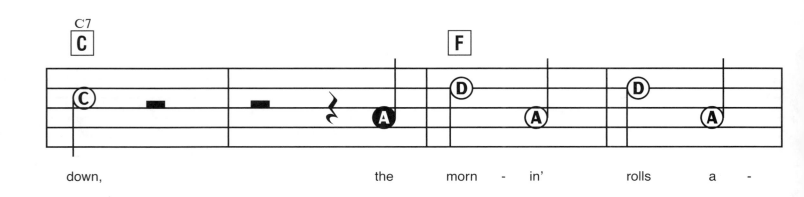

down,   the morn - in' rolls a -

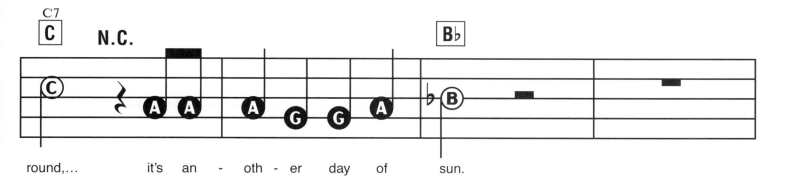

round,... it's an - oth - er day of sun.

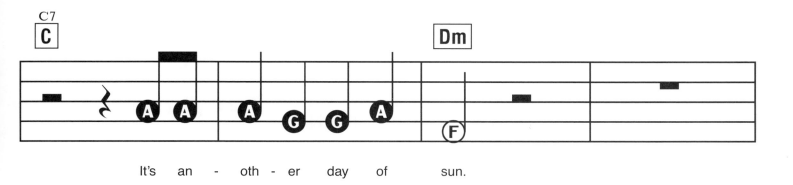

It's an - oth - er day of sun.

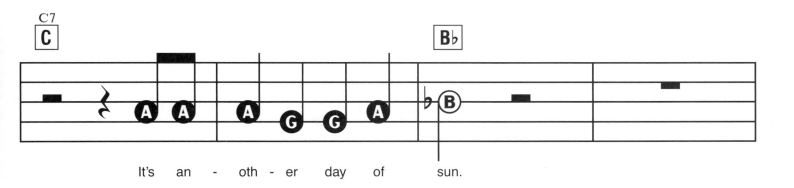

It's an - oth - er day of sun.

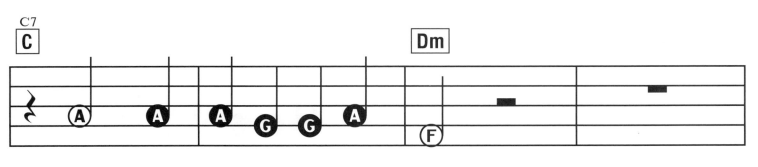

It's an - oth - er day of sun.

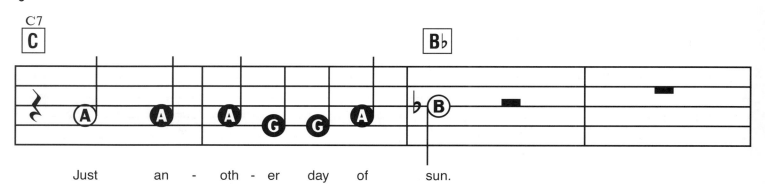

Just an - oth - er day of sun.

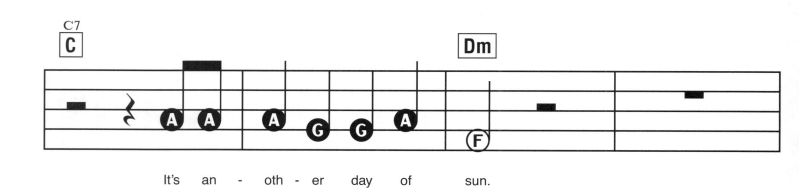

It's an - oth - er day of sun.

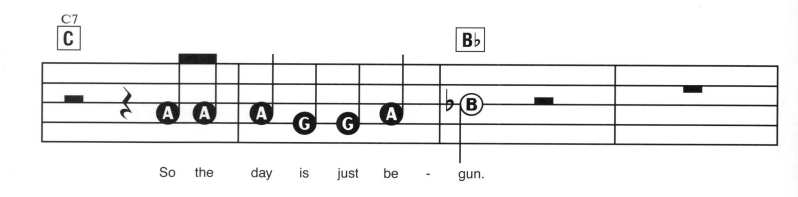

So the day is just be - gun.

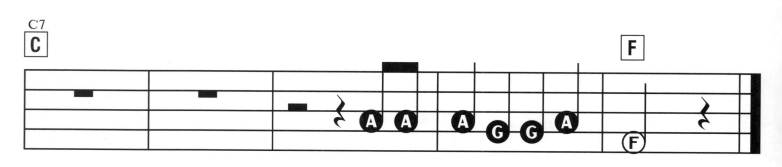

It's an - oth - er day of sun.

Mia and Sebastian's Theme

Registration 8
Rhythm: Waltz

Music by
Justin Hurwitz

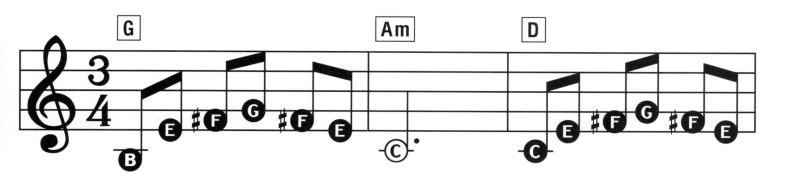

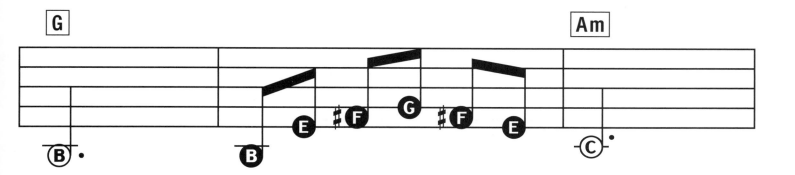

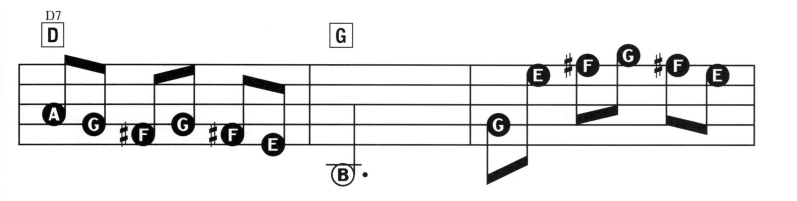

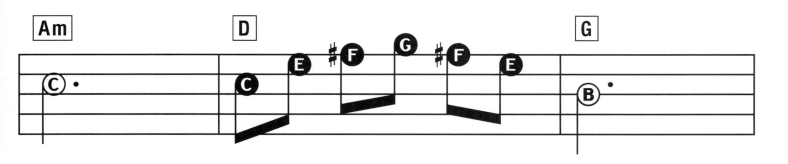

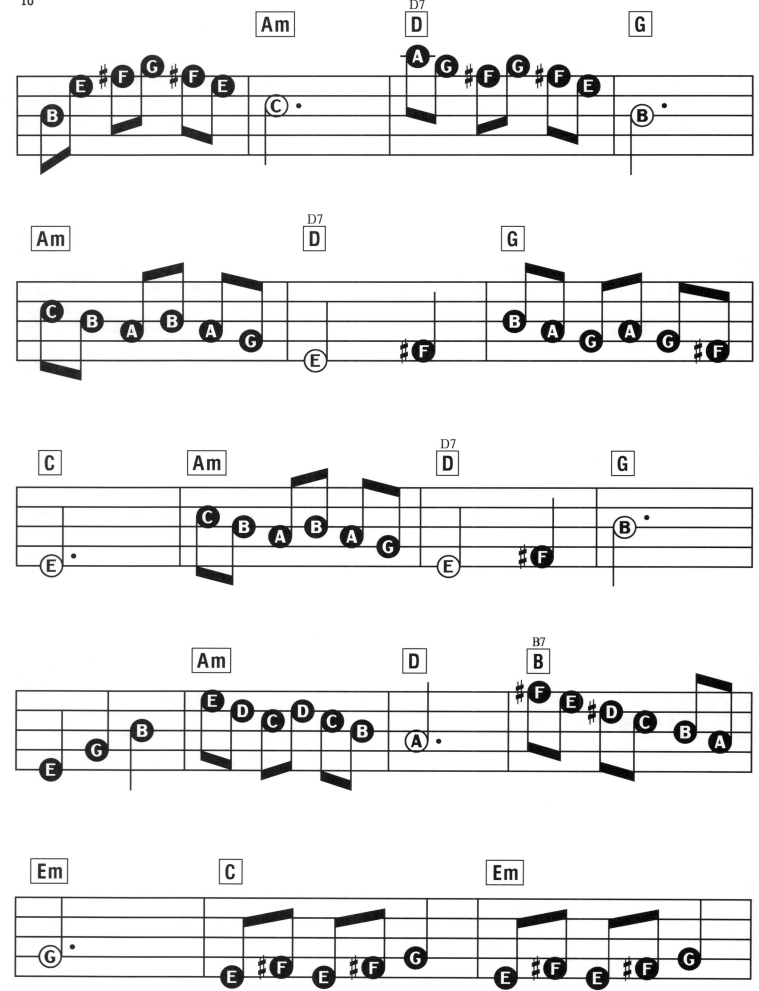

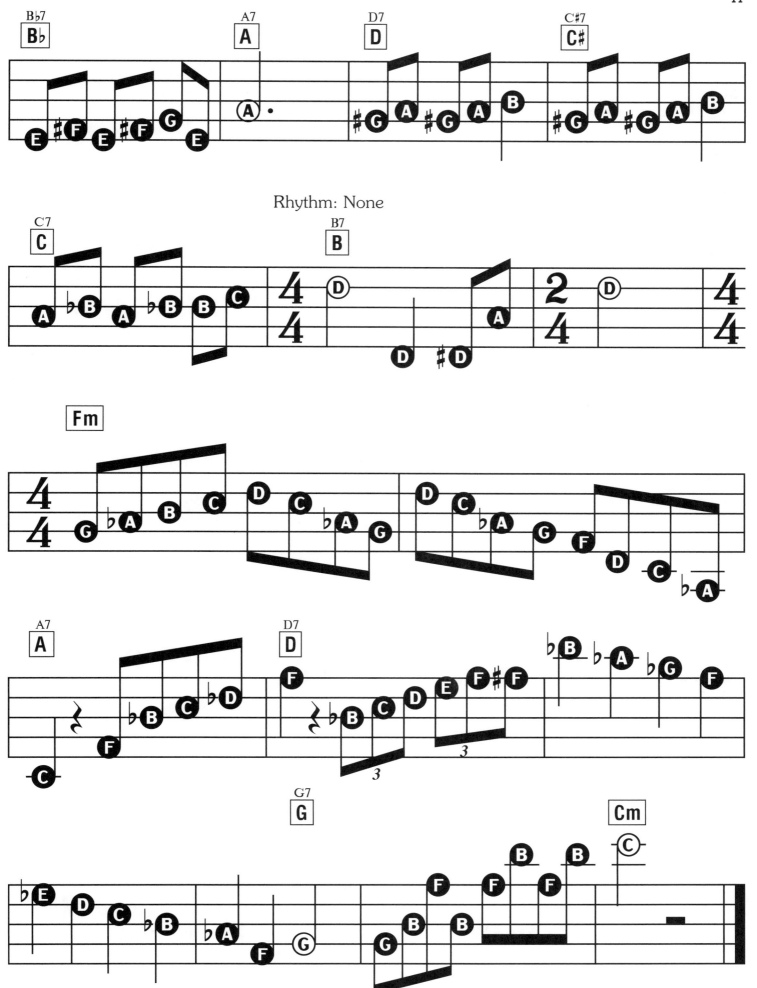

Rhythm: None

11

Someone in the Crowd

Registration 2
Rhythm: Broadway Two-Beat

Music by Justin Hurwitz
Lyrics by Benj Pasek & Justin Paul

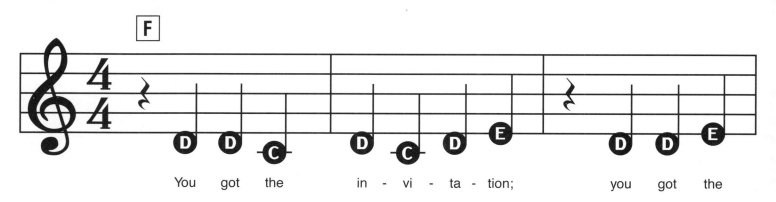

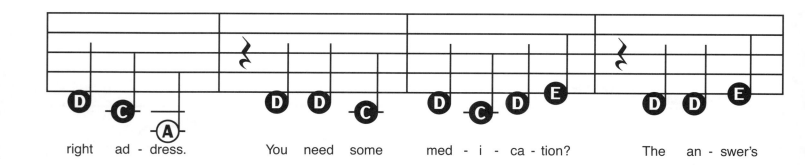

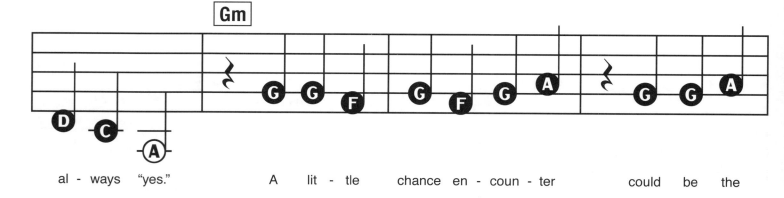

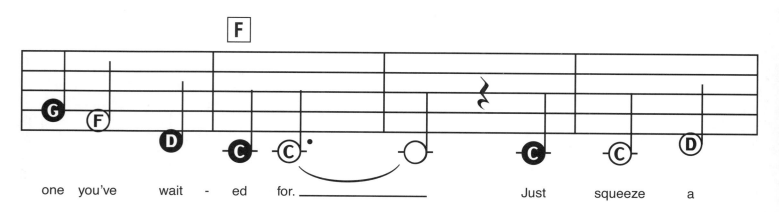

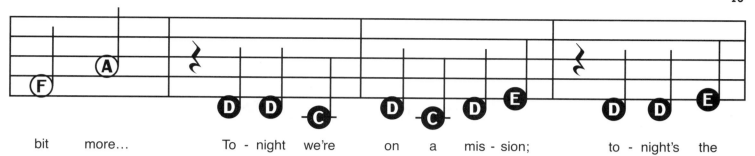

bit more…   To - night we're   on a mis - sion;   to - night's the

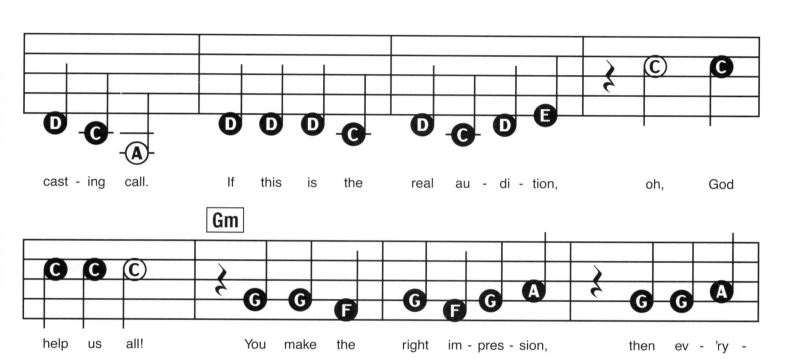

cast - ing call.   If this is the   real au - di - tion,   oh, God

Gm

help us all!   You make the   right im - pres - sion,   then ev - 'ry -

F

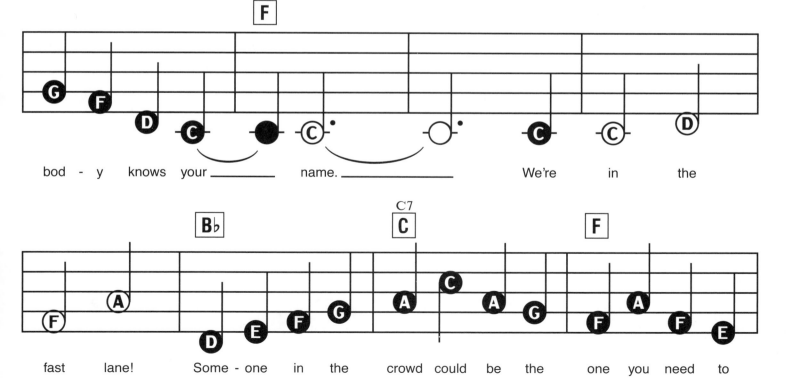

bod - y knows your _____ name. _____   We're in the

B♭   **C⁷**   **C**   **F**

fast lane!   Some - one in the   crowd could be the   one you need to

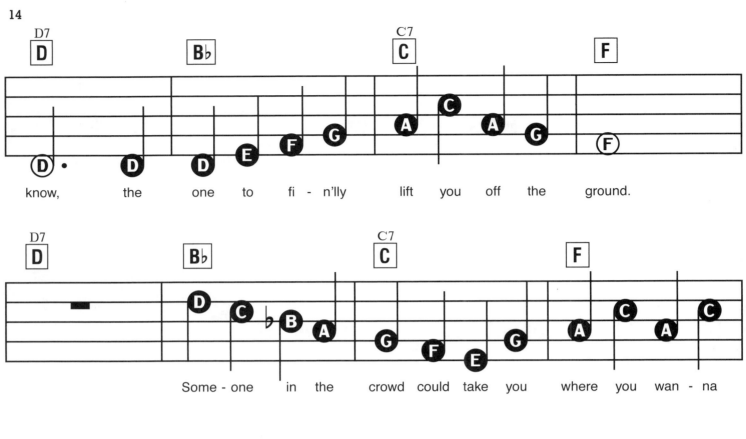

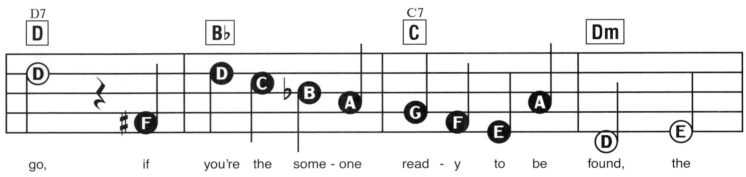

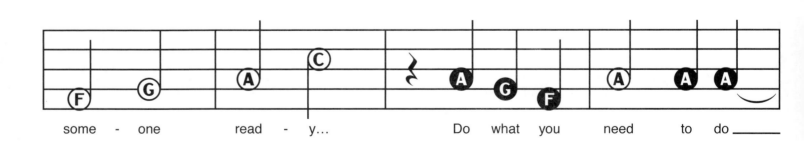

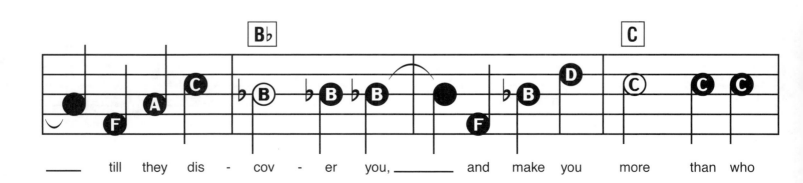

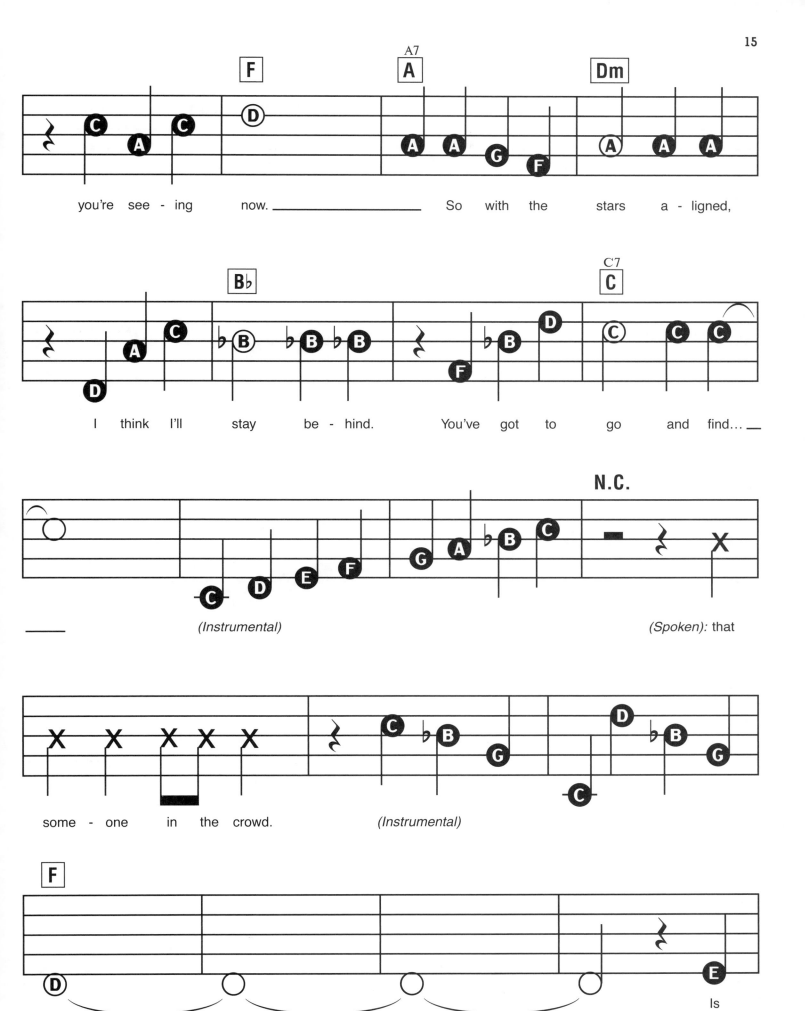

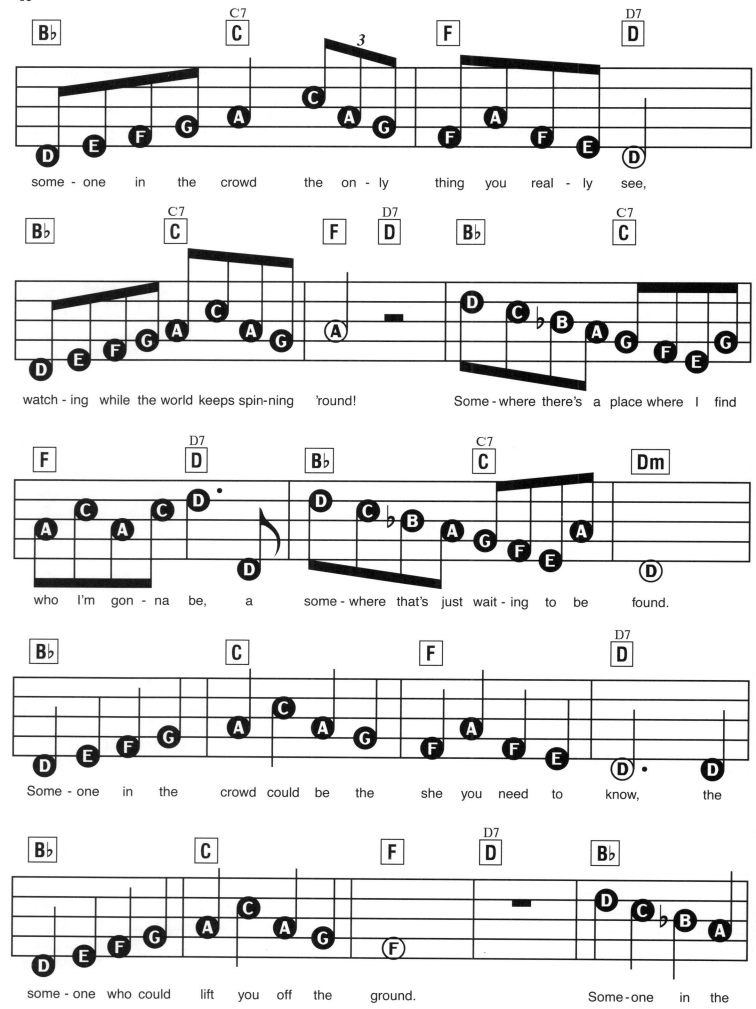

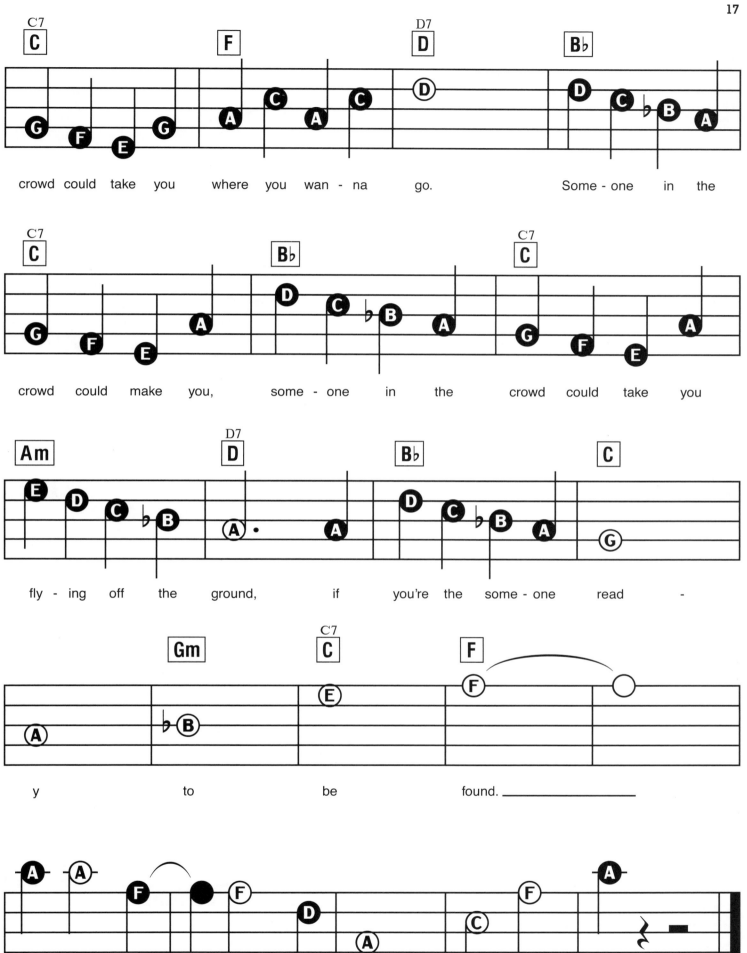

crowd could take you where you wan - na go. Some - one in the

crowd could make you, some - one in the crowd could take you

fly - ing off the ground, if you're the some - one read -

y to be found. _____

(Instrumental)

A Lovely Night

Registration 2
Rhythm: Swing

Music by Justin Hurwitz
Lyrics by Benj Pasek & Justin Paul

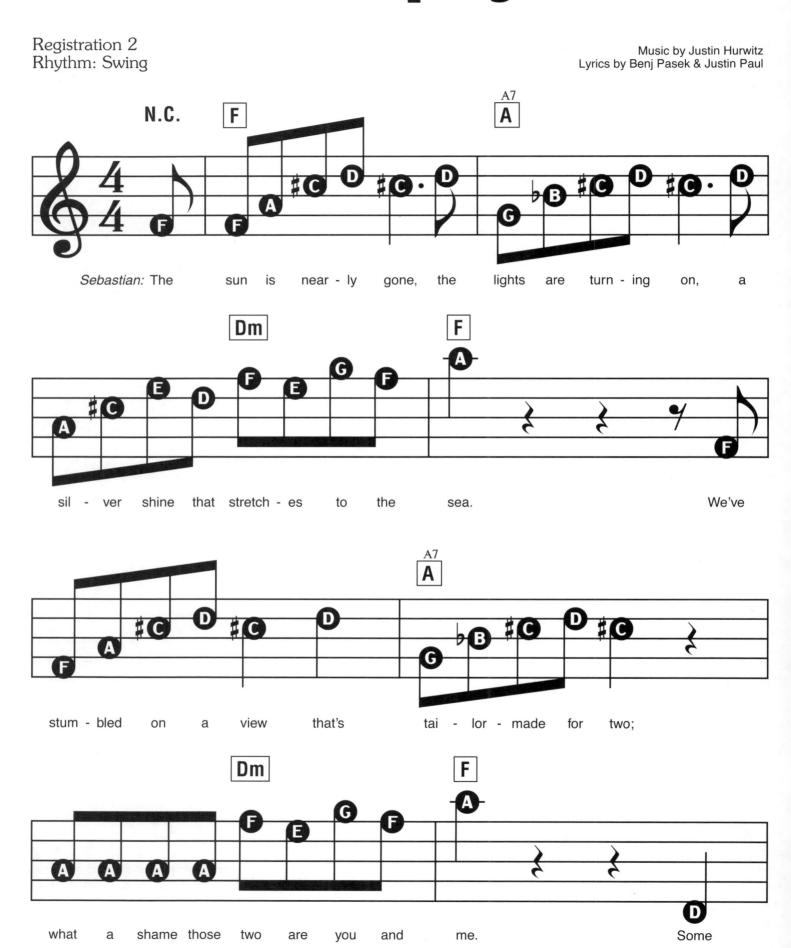

Sebastian: The sun is near-ly gone, the lights are turn-ing on, a

sil - ver shine that stretch - es to the sea. We've

stum - bled on a view that's tai - lor - made for two;

what a shame those two are you and me. Some

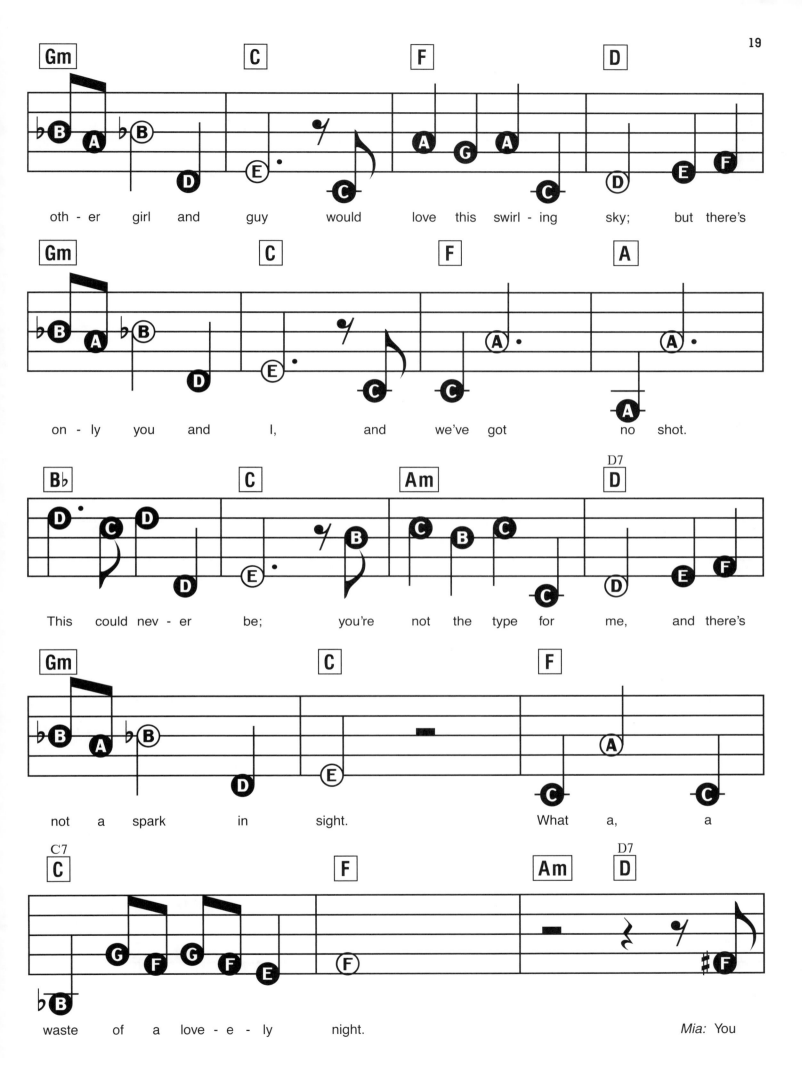

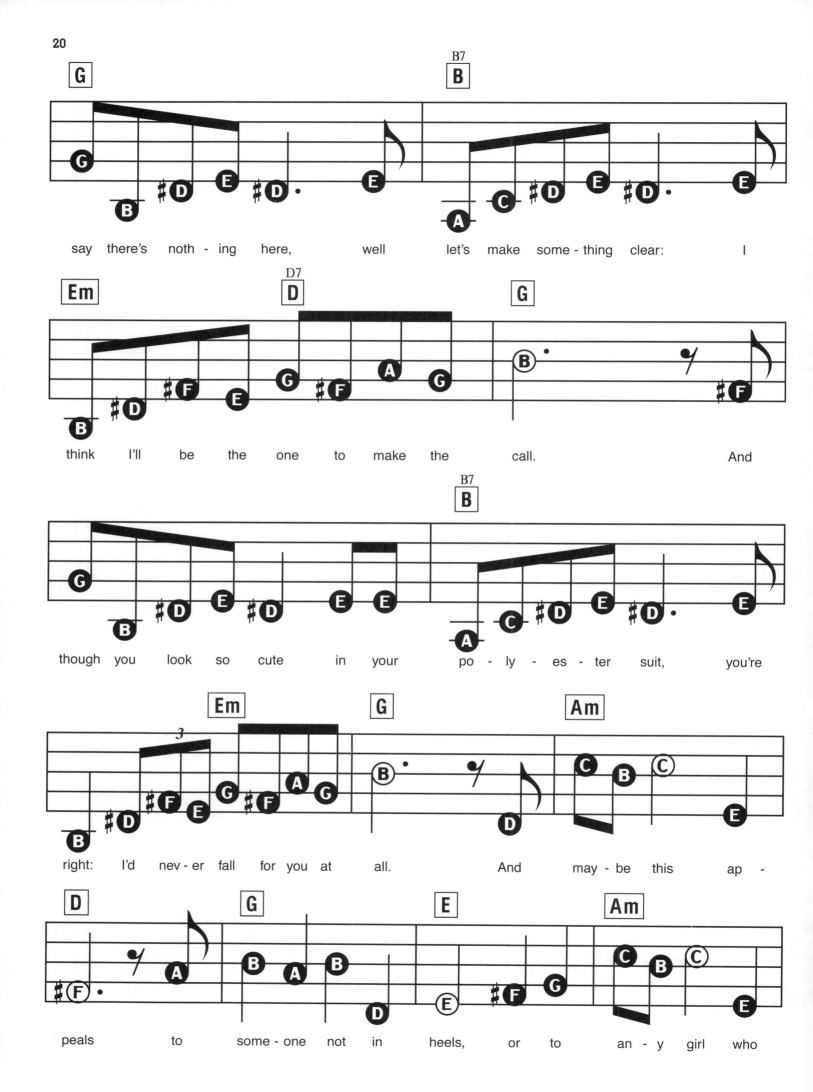

21

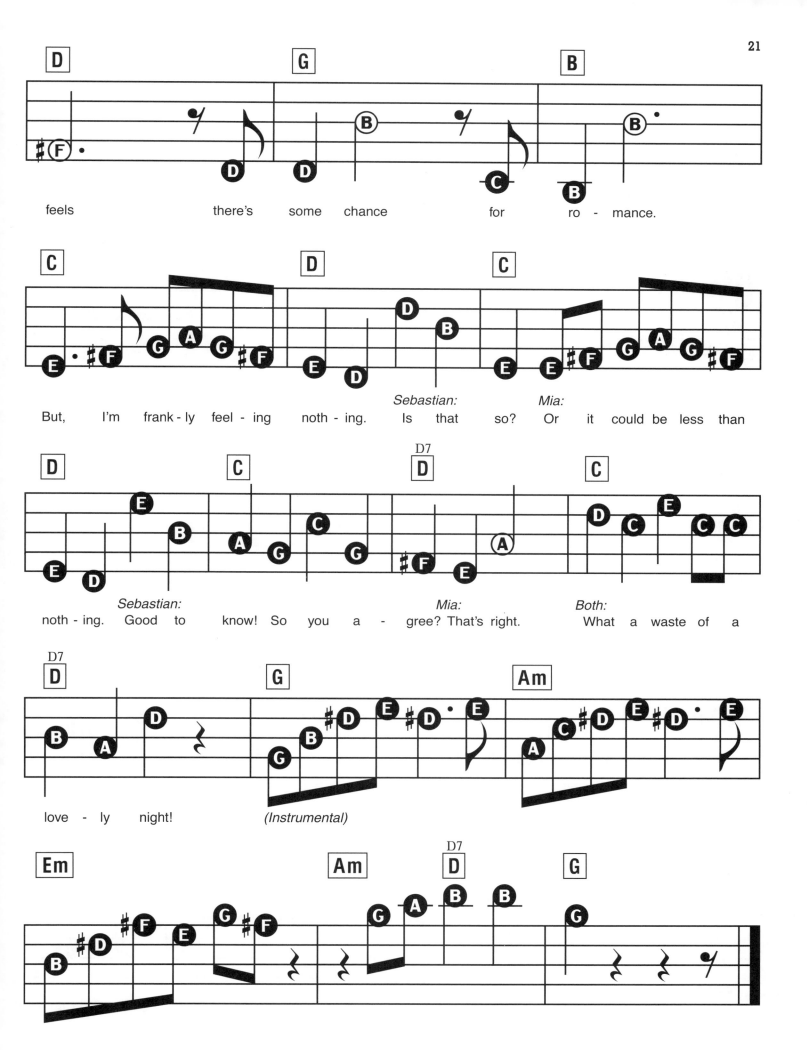

City of Stars

Registration 8
Rhythm: Ballad

Music by Justin Hurwitz
Lyrics by Benj Pasek & Justin Paul

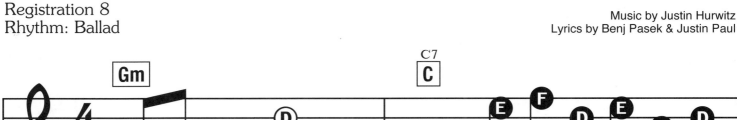

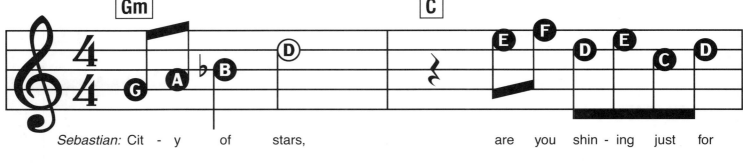

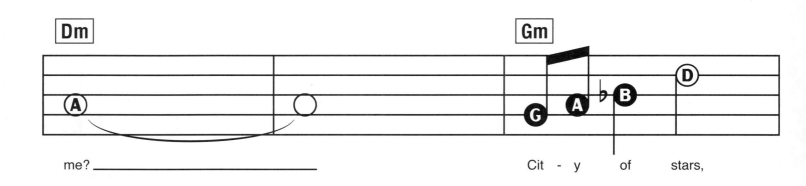

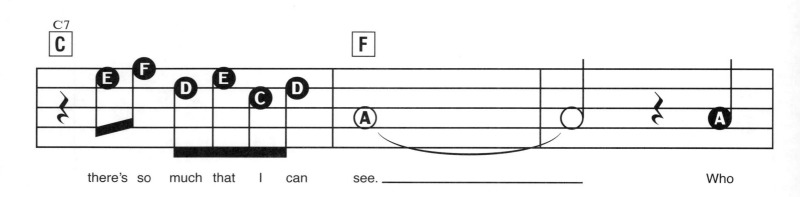

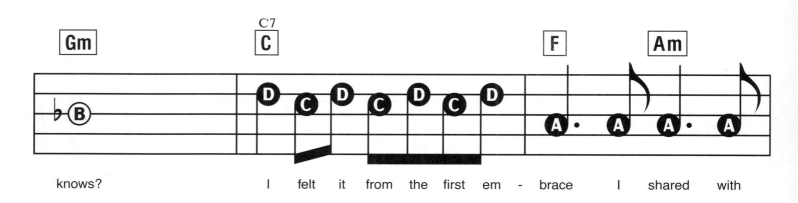

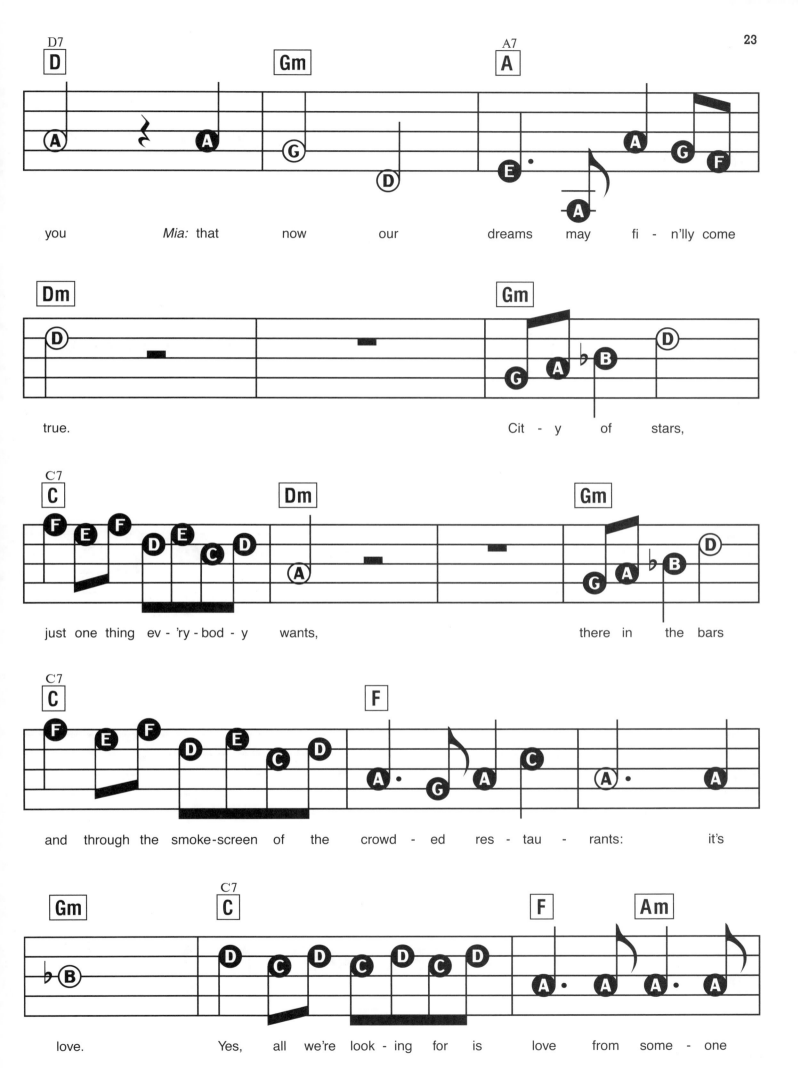

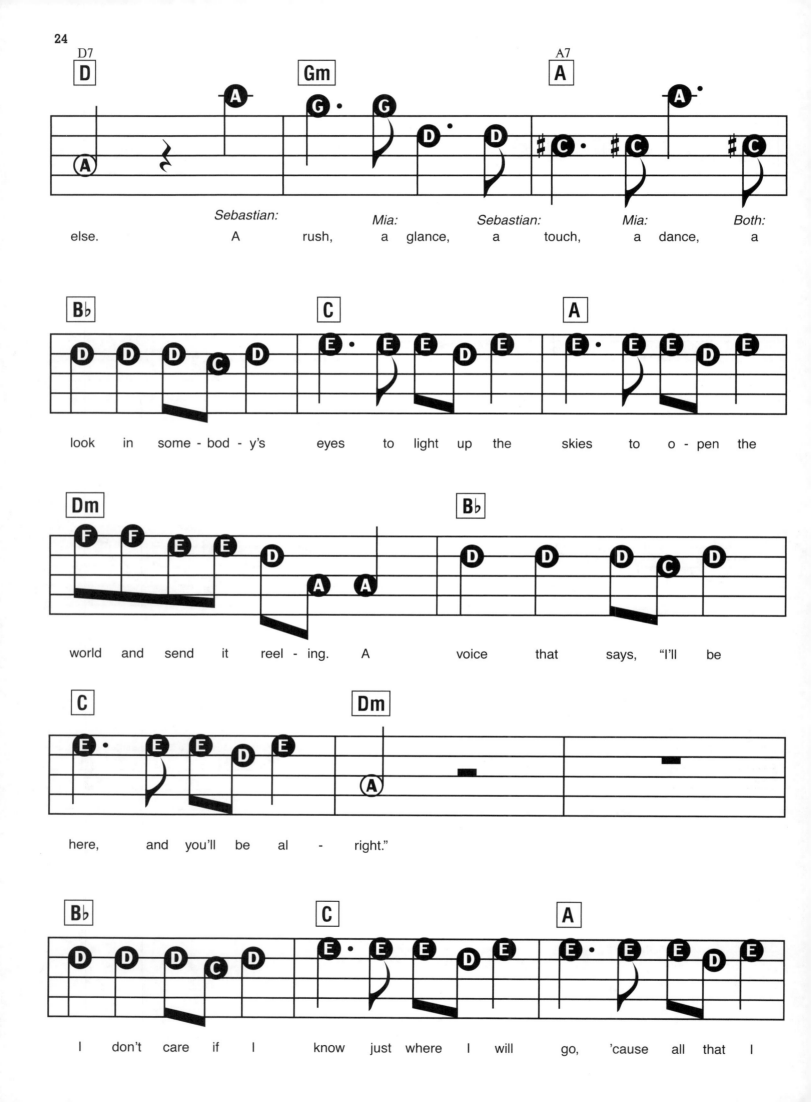

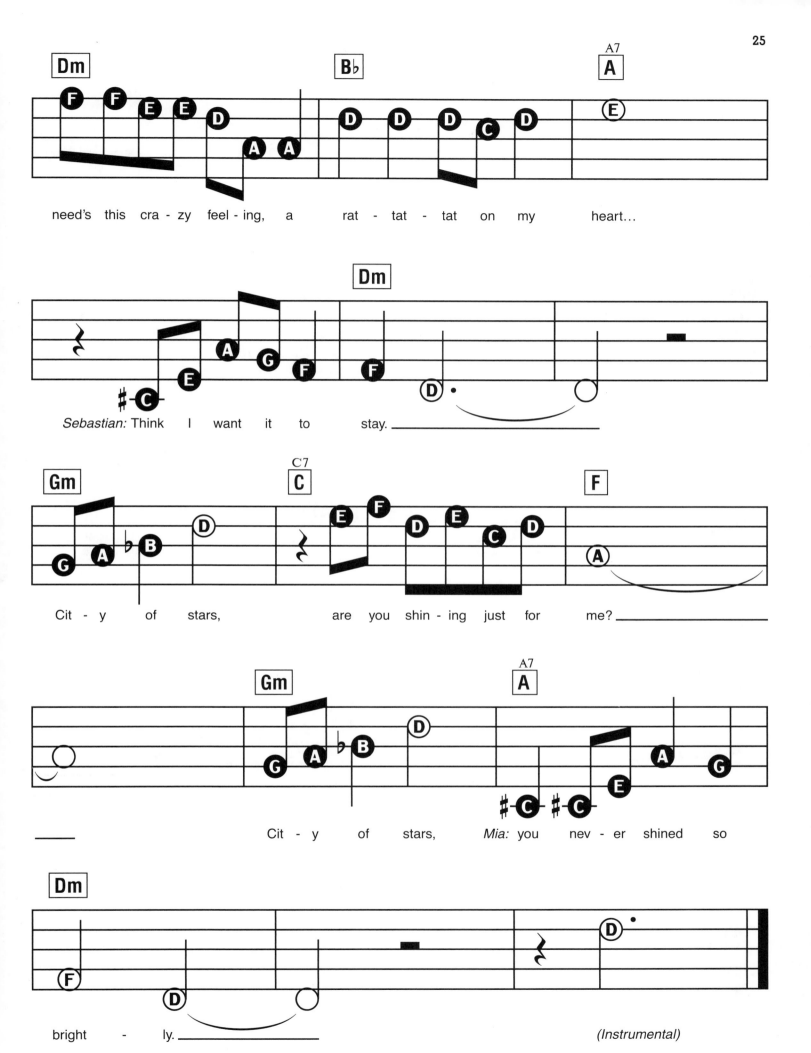

Start a Fire

Registration 2
Rhythm: Shuffle or Swing

Music & Lyrics by John Stephens,
Angélique Cinélu, Marius De Vries
and Justin Hurwitz

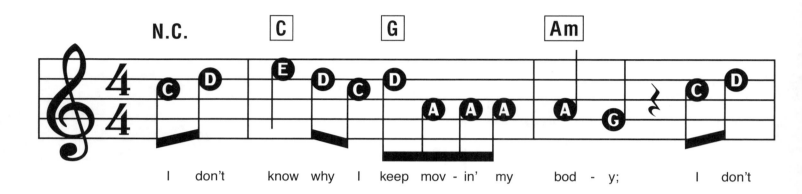

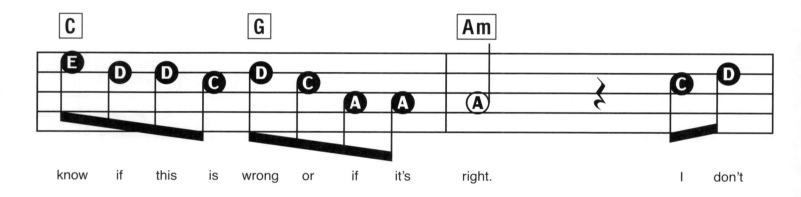

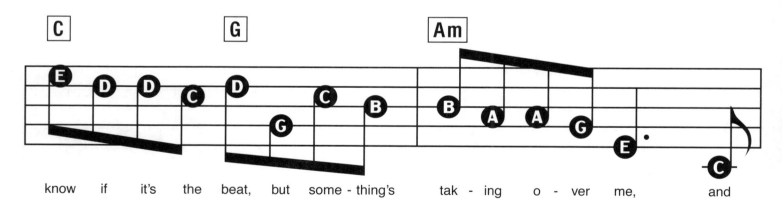

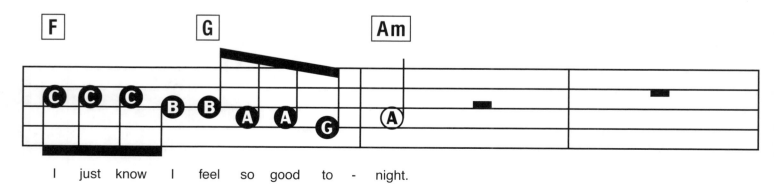

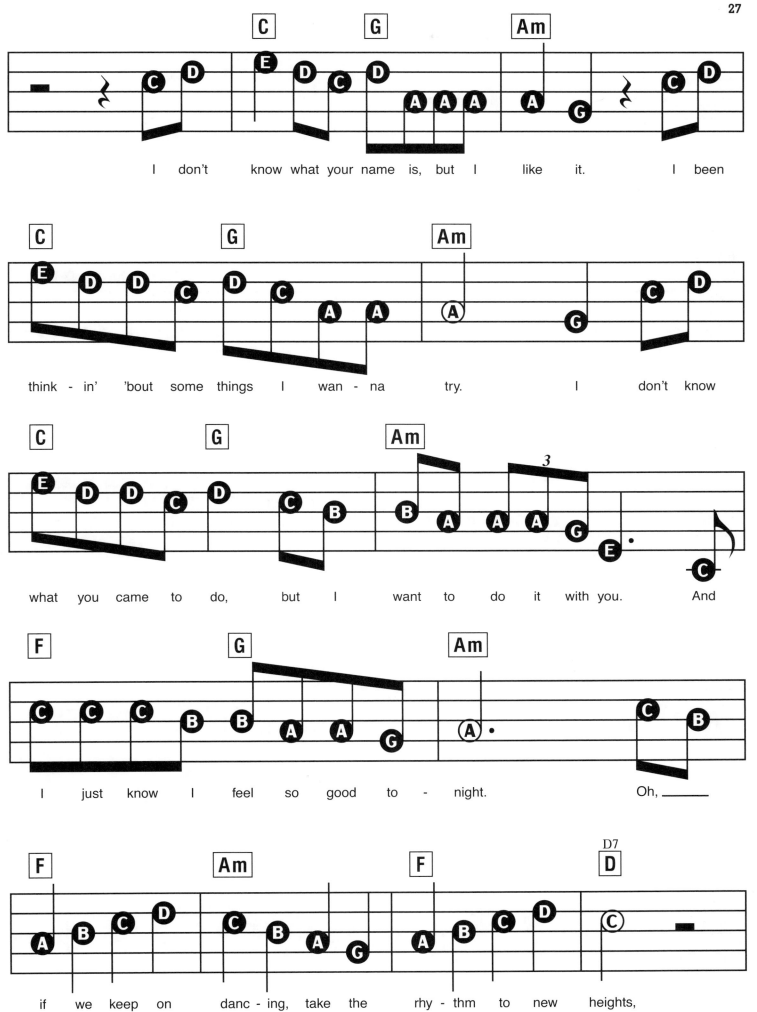

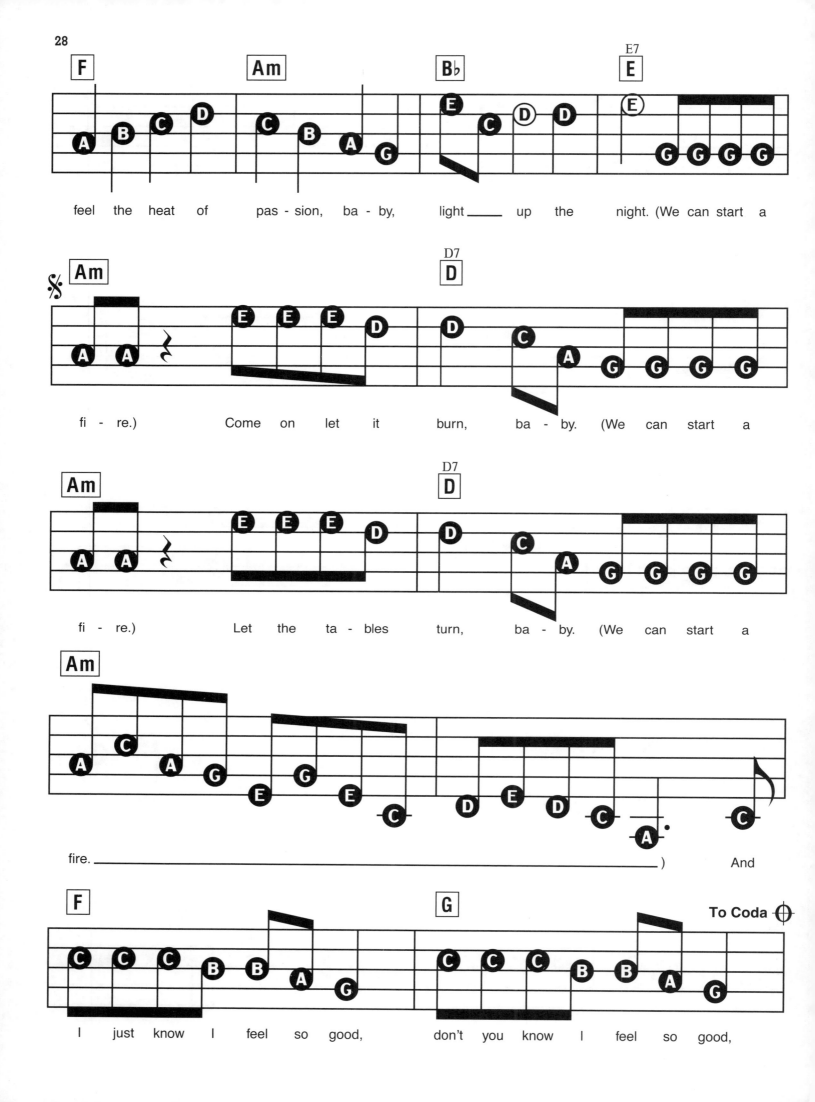

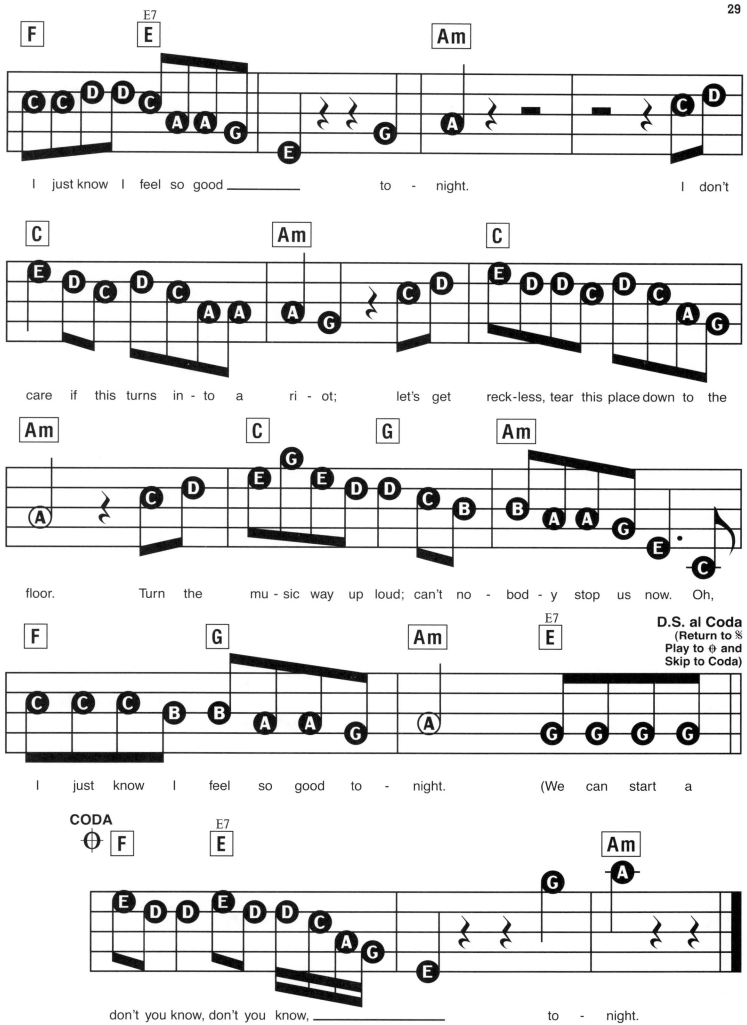

Audition
(The Fools Who Dream)

Registration 8
Rhythm: Waltz

Music by Justin Hurwitz
Lyrics by Benj Pasek & Justin Paul

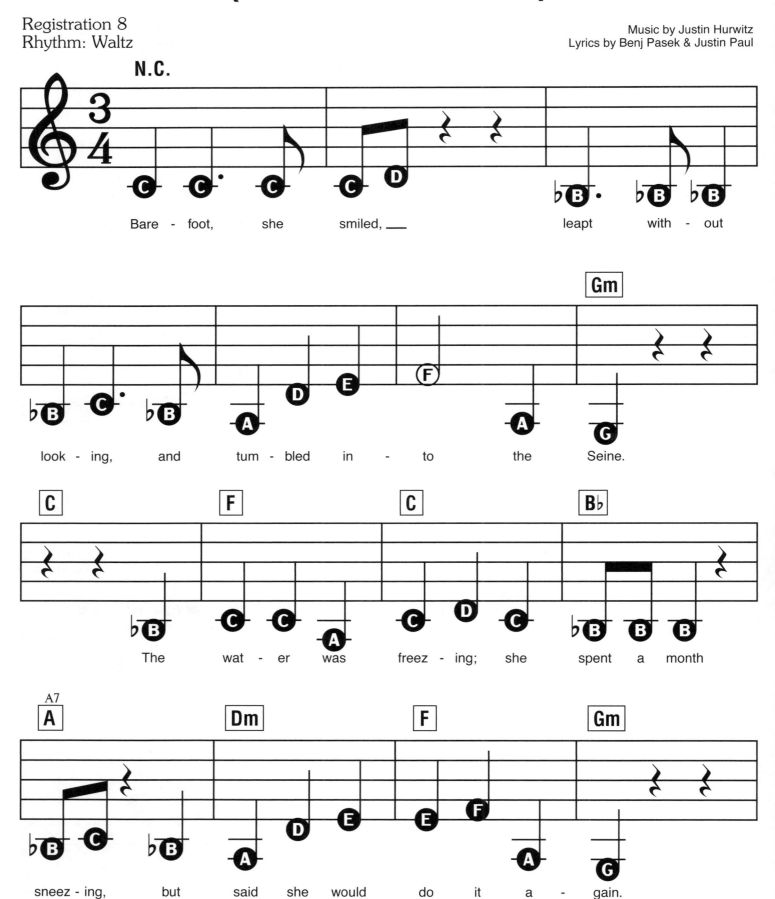

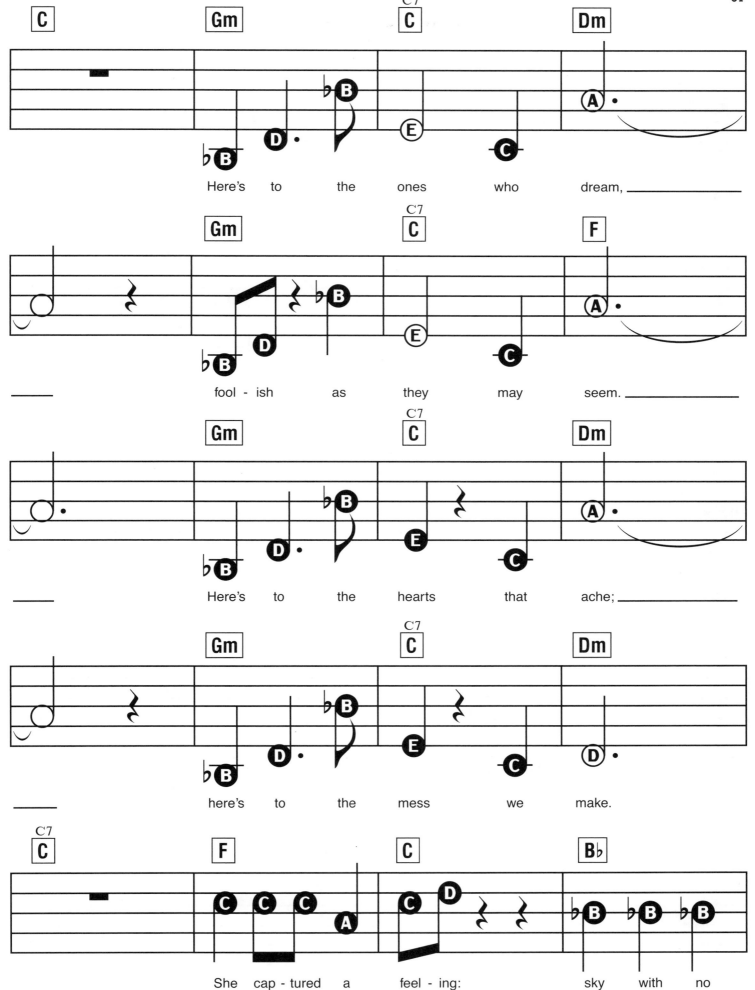

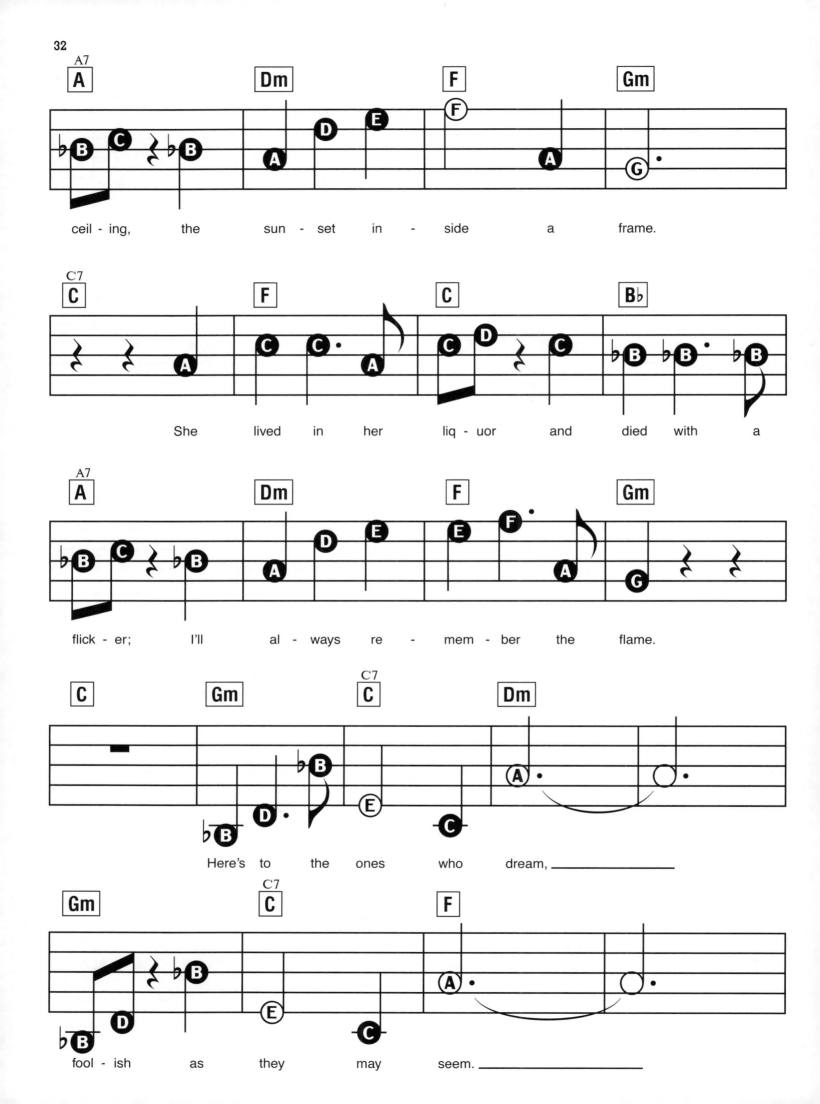

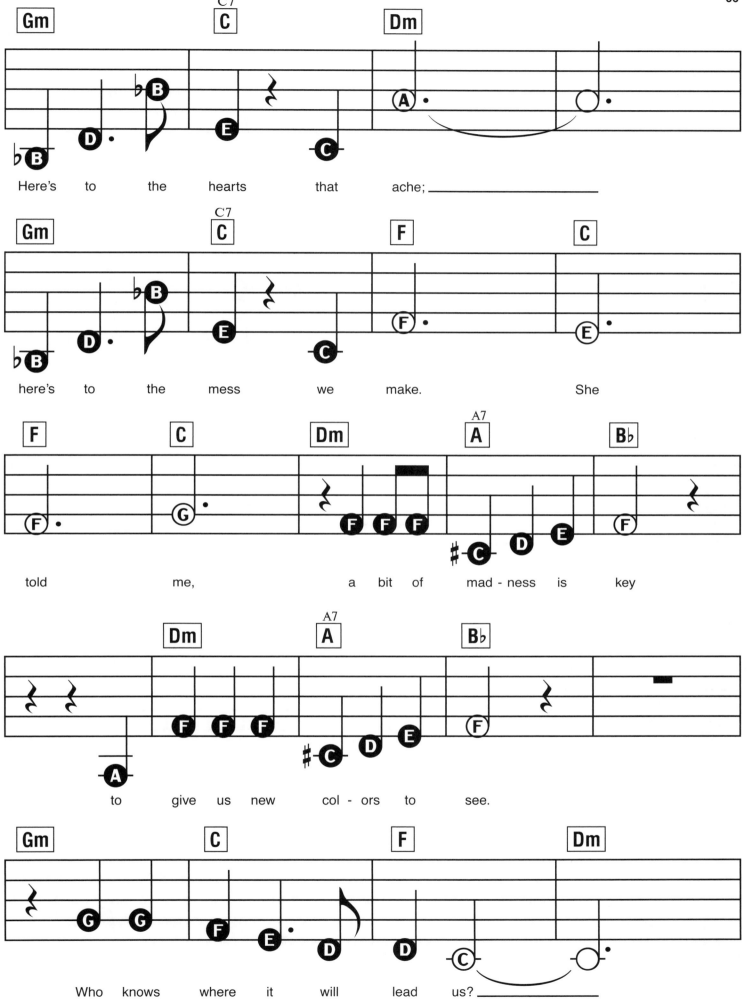

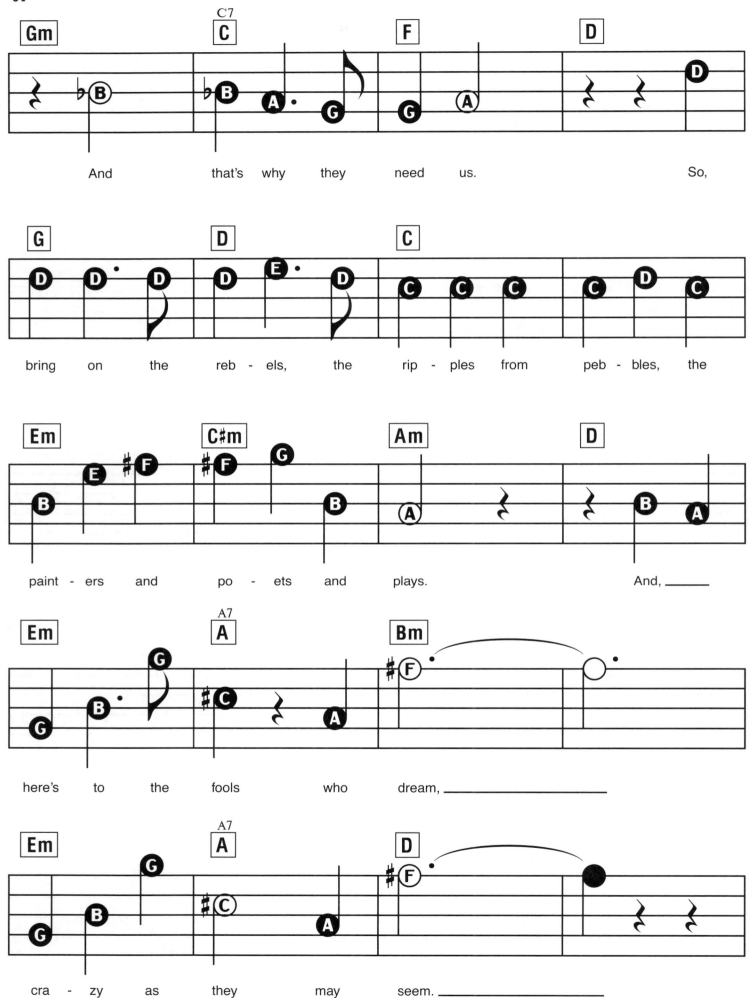

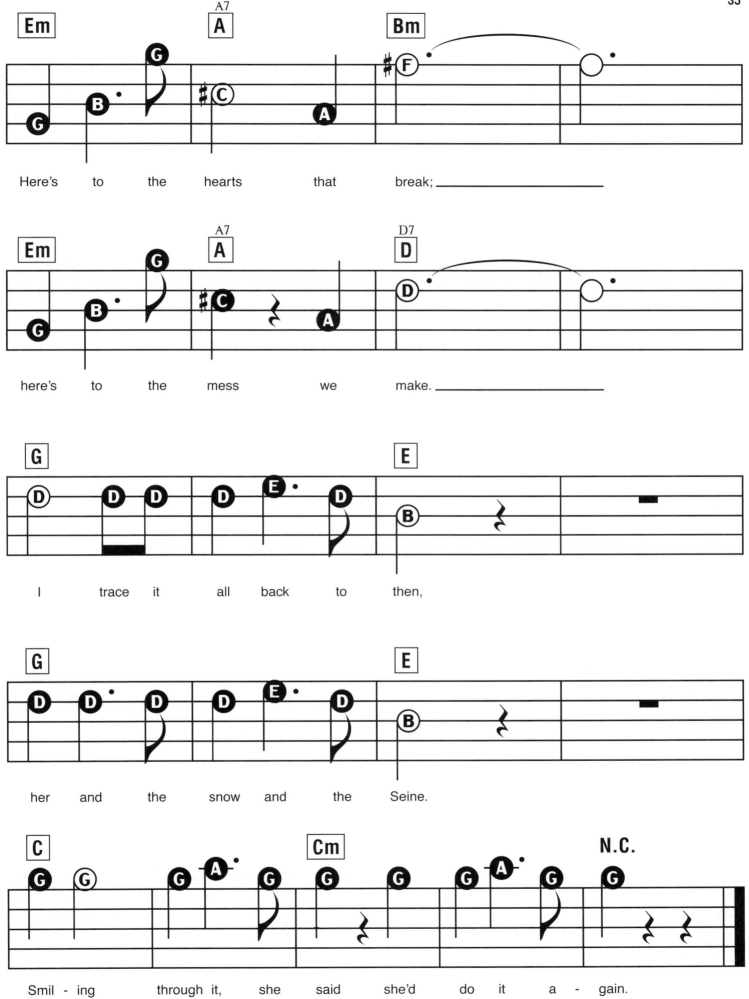

Epilogue

Registration 2
Rhythm: None

Music by
Justin Hurwitz

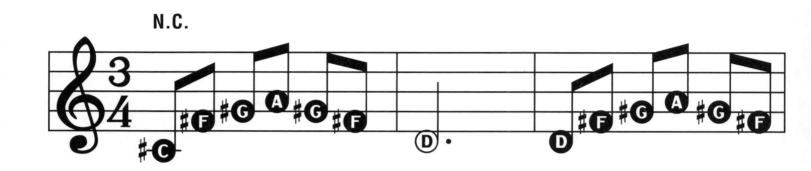

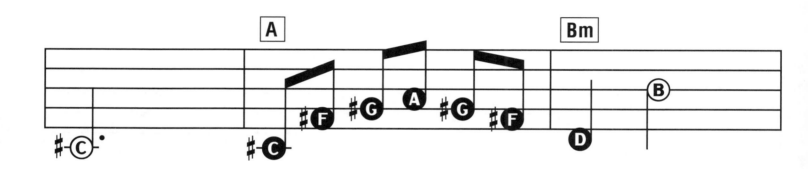

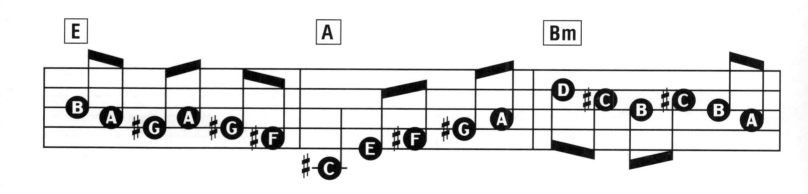

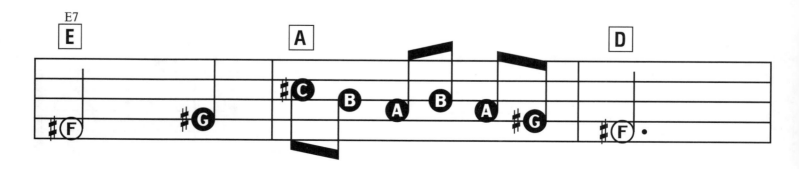

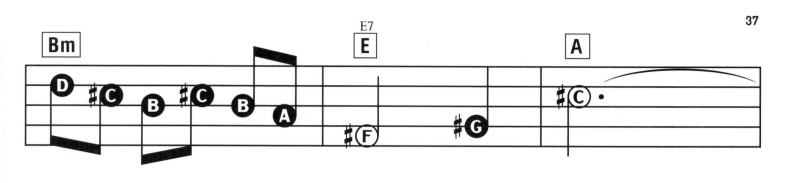

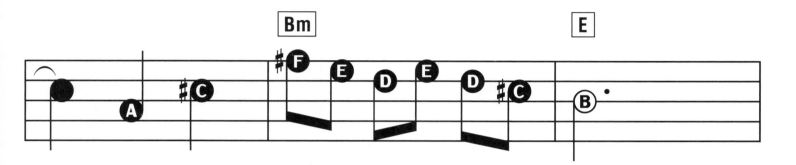

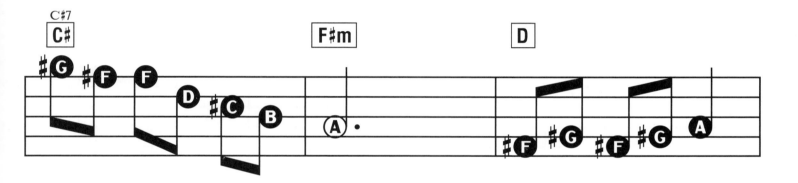

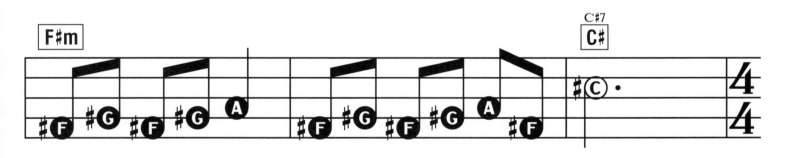

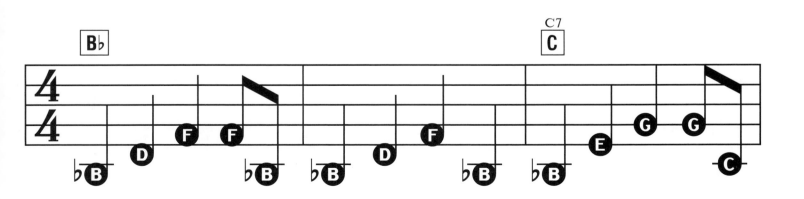

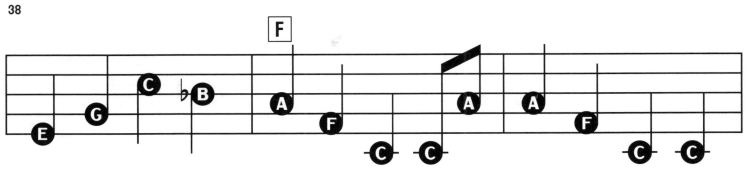

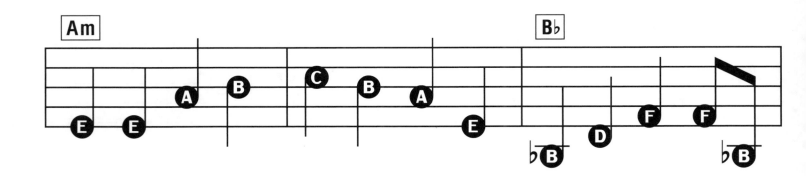

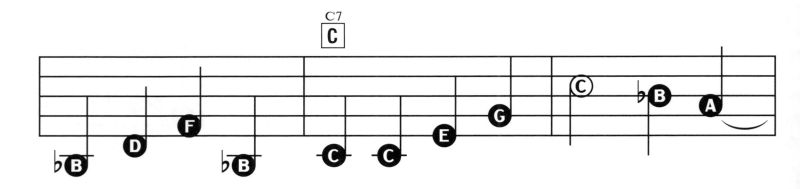

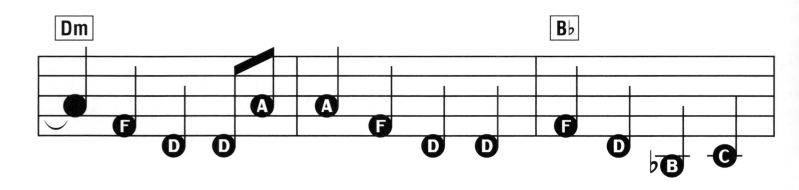

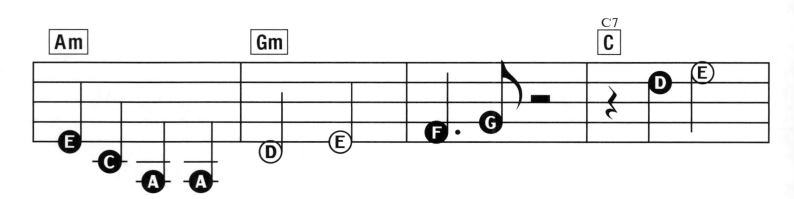

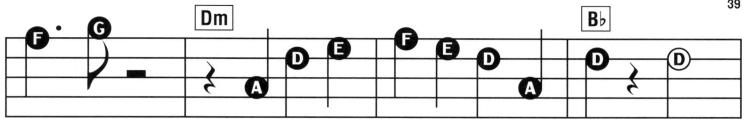
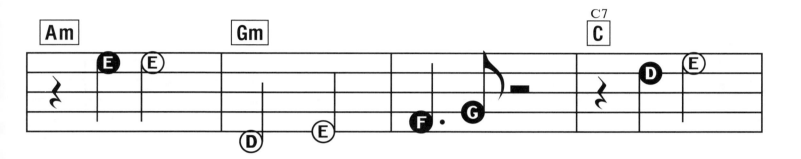
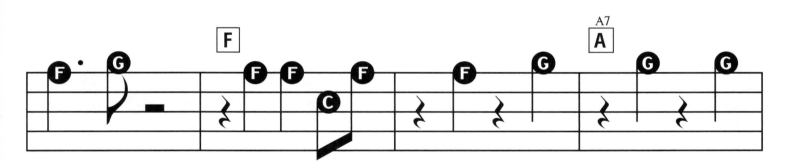
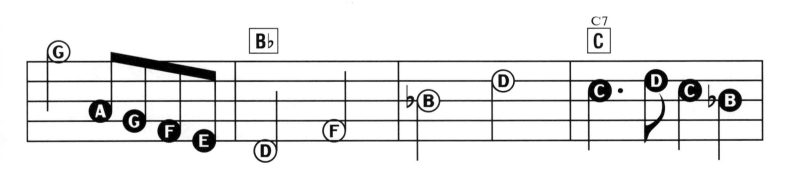
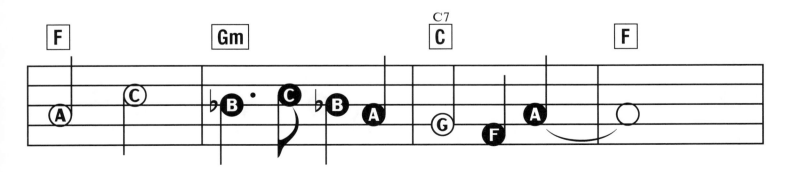

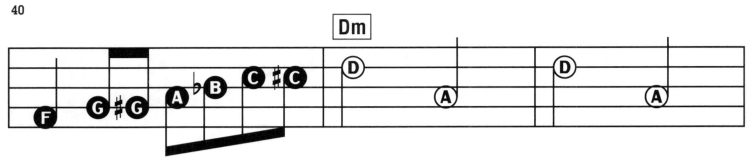

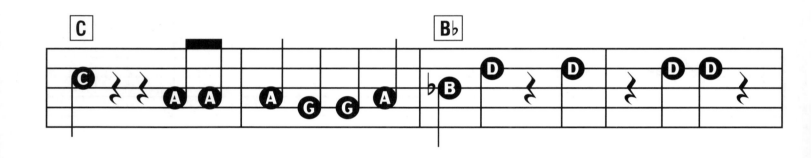

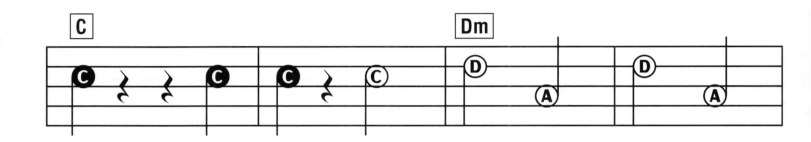

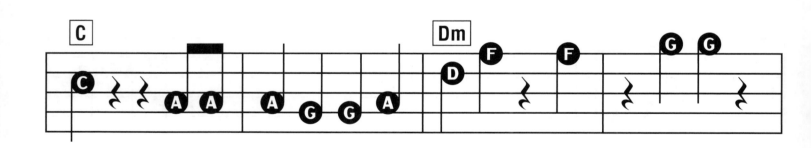

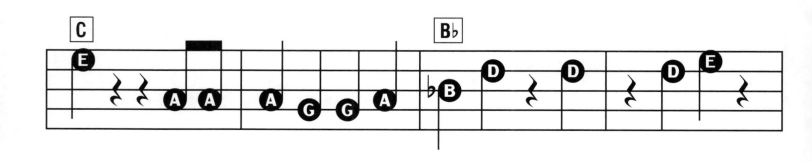

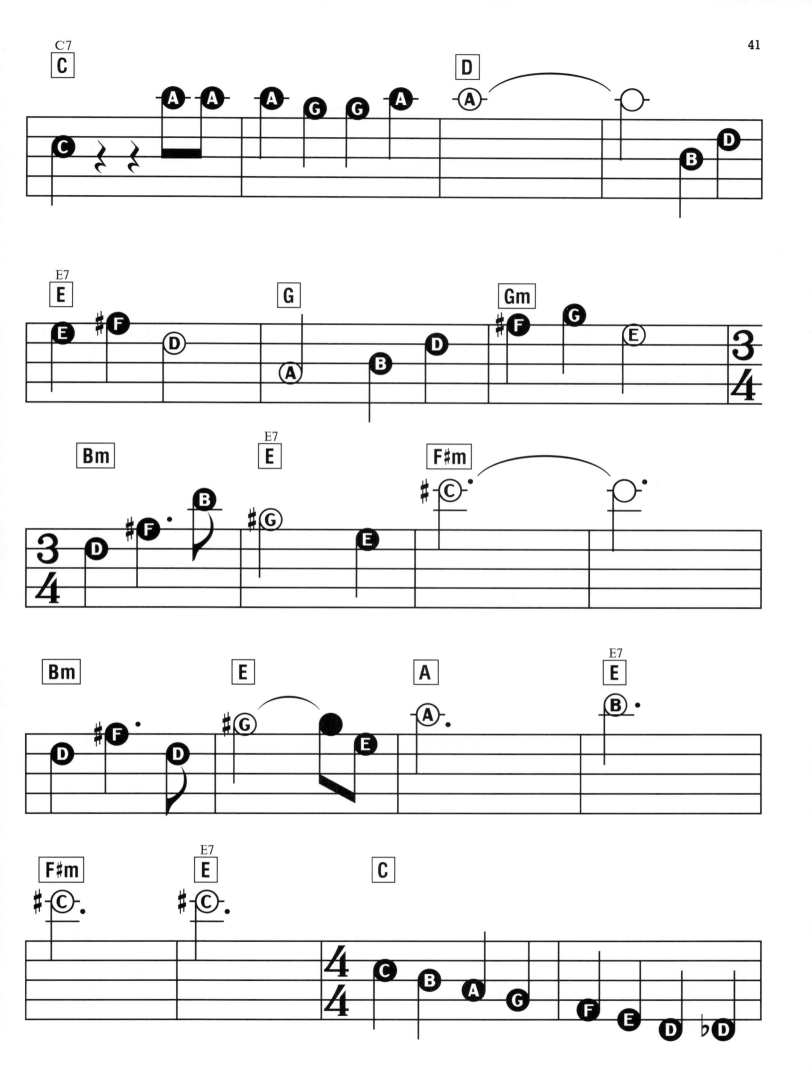

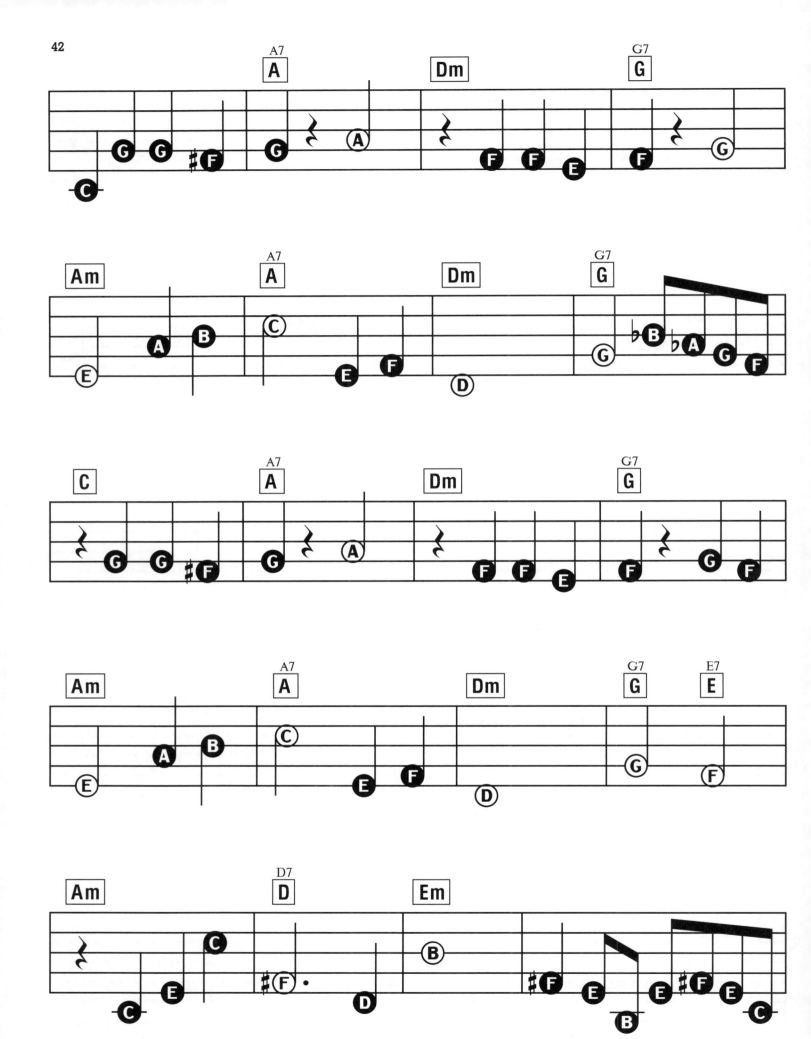

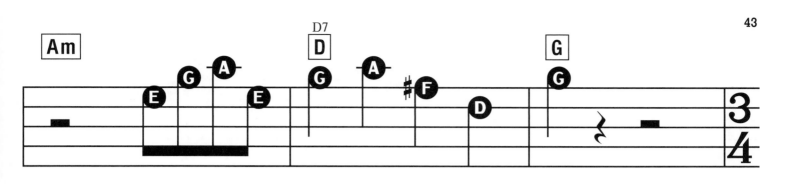

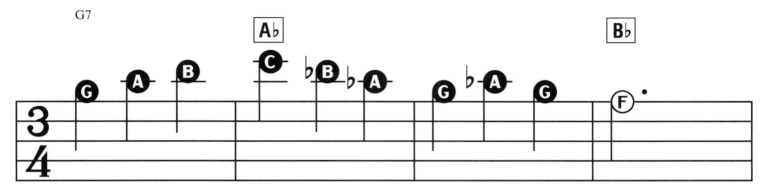

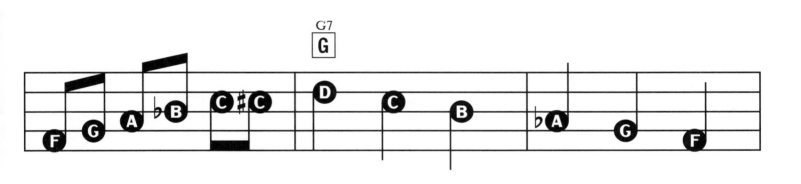

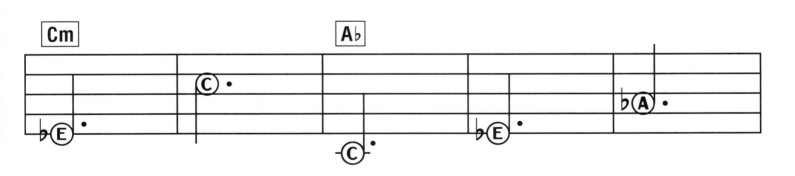

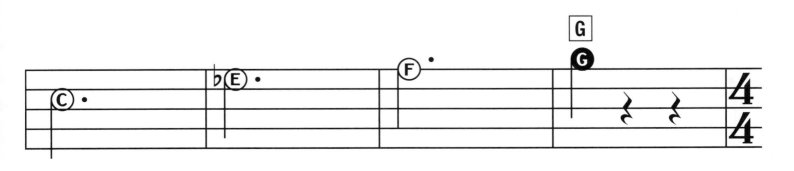

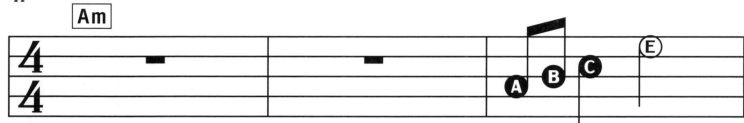

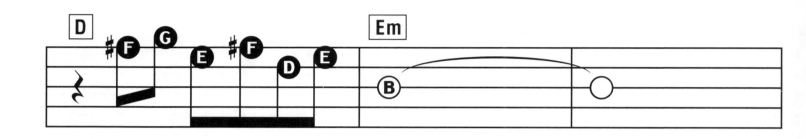

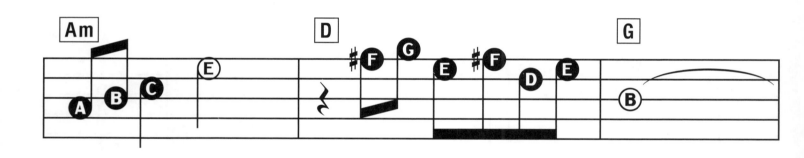

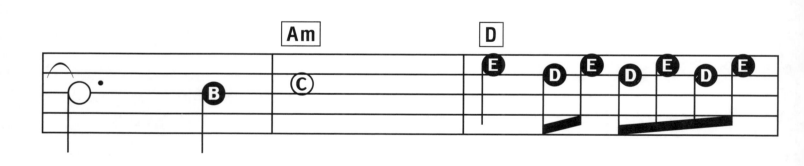

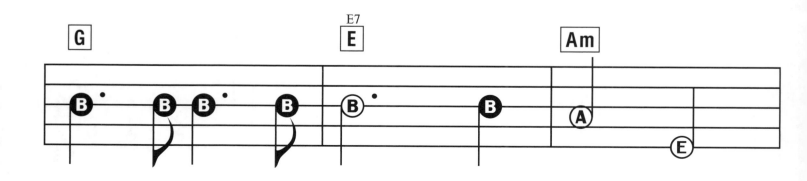

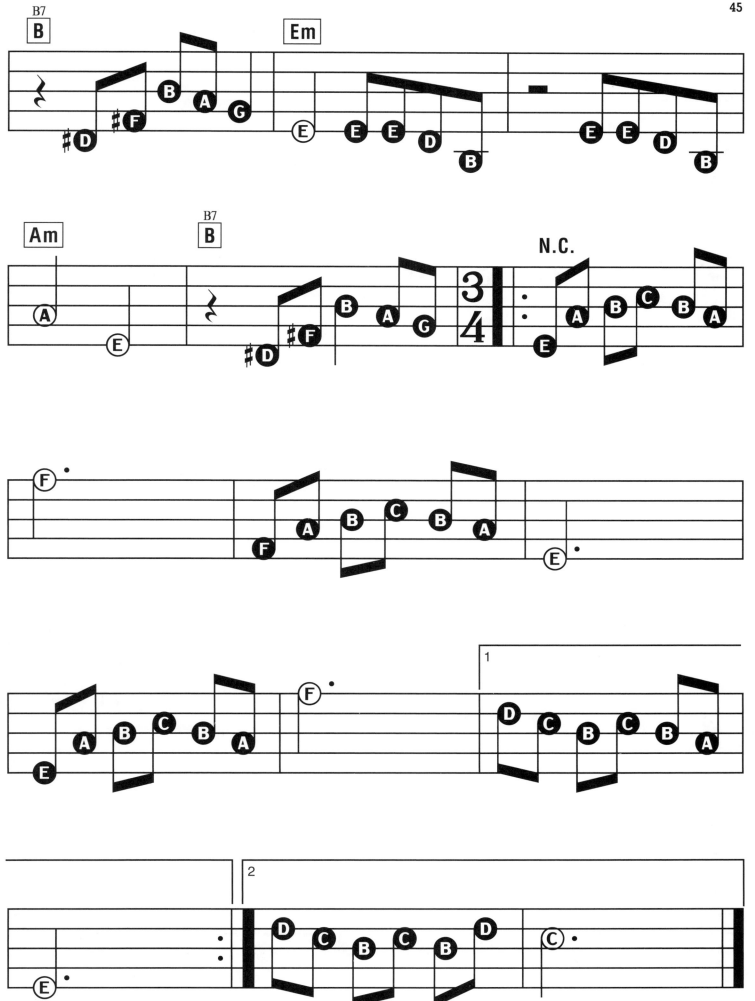

Engagement Party

Registration 8
Rhythm: Ballad

Music by
Justin Hurwitz

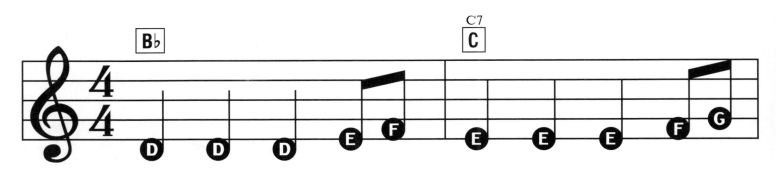

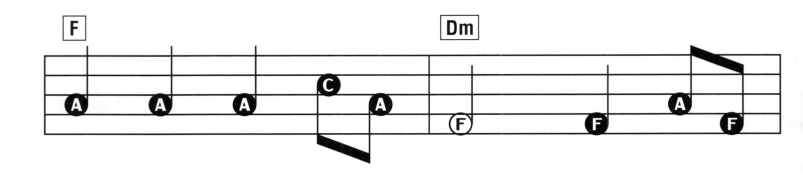

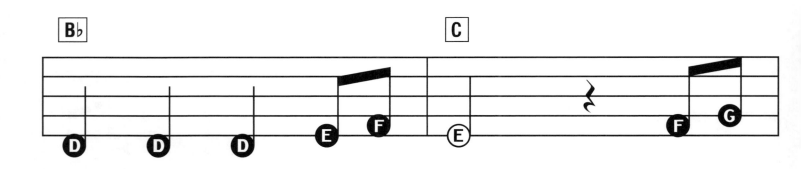

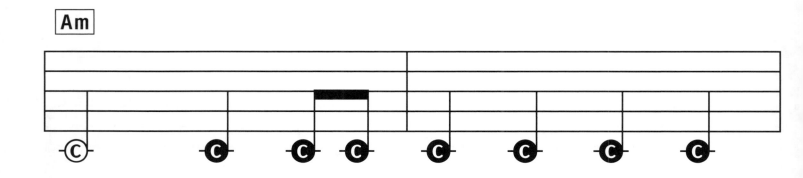

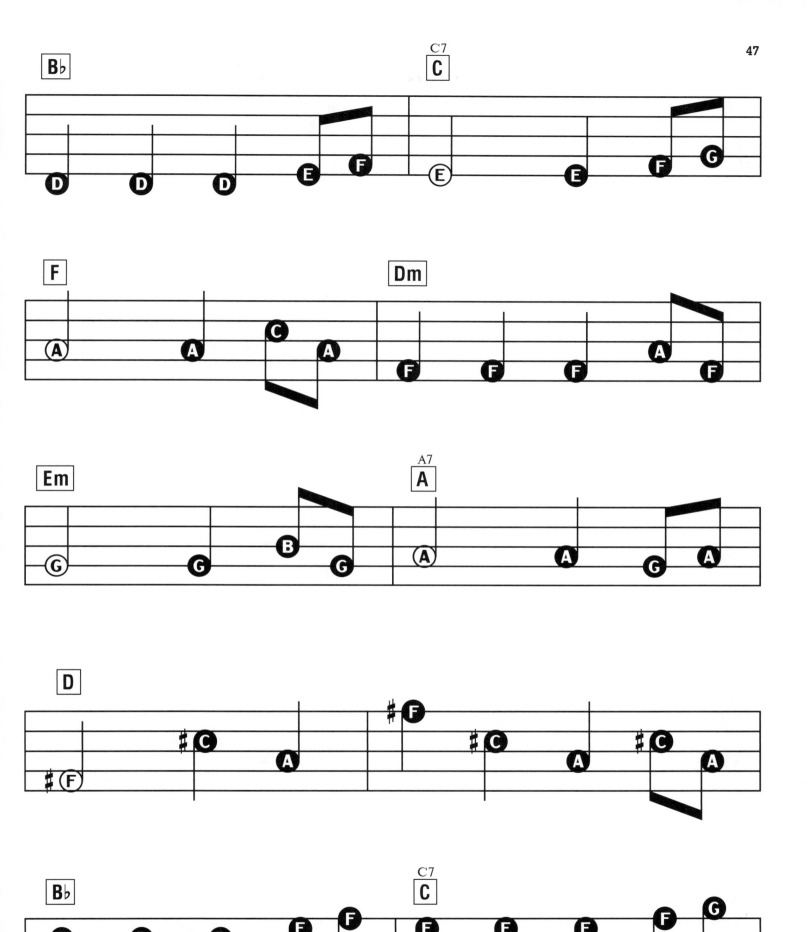

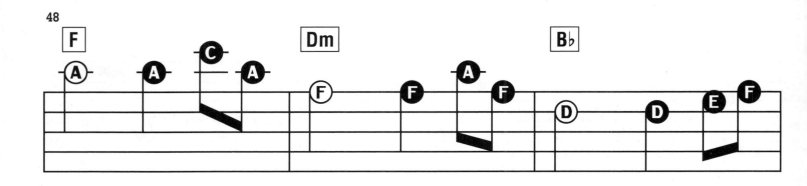

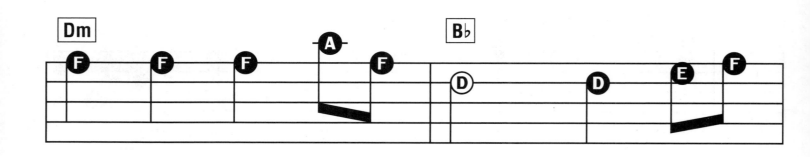

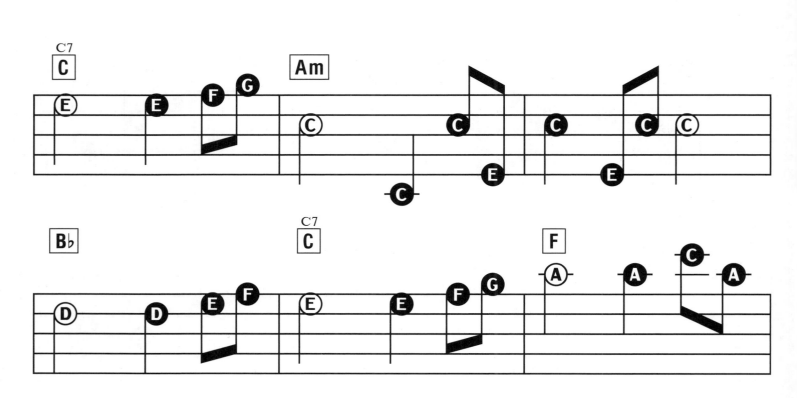

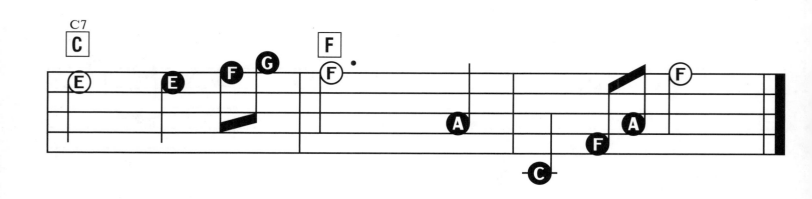